Marketing Workbook for Nonprofit Organizations
Volume I: Develop the Plan

Second Edition

by Gary J. Stern
with *Web Wisdom* by Elana Centor

FIELDSTONE
ALLIANCE

SAINT PAUL
MINNESOTA

Fieldstone Alliance is committed to strengthening the performance of the nonprofit sector. Through the synergy of its consulting, training, publishing, and research and demonstration projects, Fieldstone Alliance provides solutions to issues facing nonprofits, funders, and the communities they serve. Fieldstone Alliance was formerly Wilder Publishing and Wilder Consulting departments of the Amherst H. Wilder Foundation. For information about other Fieldstone Alliance publications, see the last pages of this book. If you would like more information about Fieldstone Alliance and our services, please contact Fieldstone Alliance at

800-274-6024
www.FieldstoneAlliance.org

Edited by Vincent Hyman
Designed by Rebecca Andrews
Illustrated by Giora Carmi

Special thanks to Rebecca Andrews, Emil Angelica, Joe Bergen, Elana Centor, Scot Covey, Gayle Cupit, Claudia Dengler, Vince Hyman, Dr. K, Sandra Larson, Delia Naughton, Tom Olson, Ellen Sue Stern, Michael Winer, The Drucker Foundation, and the American Lung Associations of Texas and Arizona/New Mexico.

Manufactured in the United States of America
Third printing, September 2008

Library of Congress Cataloging-in-Publication Data

Stern, Gary J. (Gary John), 1953-
    Markting workbook for nonprofit organizations / by Gary J. Stern. ;
with web widsom by Elana Centor.--Rev. and updated ed.
        p. cm.
    Includes bibliographical references.
    Contents: v. 1. Develop the plan
    ISBN 13: 978-1-63026-375-1

    1. Nonprofit Organizations--Marketing. I. Centor, Elana. II. Title.

HF5415 .S768 2001
658.8--dc21

                                                                2001018863

This book is dedicated to my father, Lester A. Stern,
a wonderful man and marketer par excellence.

About the Authors

GARY J. STERN is president of Stern Consulting International, specializing in social sector strategy, marketing, and organizational performance. In addition to this book, which was adapted as the official marketing workbook of United Way of America, he is the author of *Marketing Workbook Volume II: Mobilize People for Marketing Success.* Gary coauthored, with Peter F. Drucker, the revised edition of the *Drucker Foundation Self-Assessment Tool* and leads the Drucker Foundation Training Team.

Formerly senior consultant with the Amherst H. Wilder Foundation, Gary J. Stern is a noted speaker and trainer. He has presented at the Stanford University Graduate School of Business, at Drucker Foundation Leadership and Management Conferences, for the United Way of Canada–Centraide Canada, and Fundacion Compromiso of Argentina. Stern International clients include the American Lung Association, National Council of Jewish Women, the Dave Thomas Foundation for Adoption, Josephson Institute of Ethics, and the Alliance for Nonprofit Management.

ELANA CENTOR is president of Elana Centor &, a marketing communications consulting firm specializing in process facilitation and traditional and e-business strategy and marketing. Prior to starting her own firm in 1997, Elana headed up the interactive group for Rapp Collins Communications, consulting with Rapp Collins clients worldwide on web marketing.

Elana has received professional recognition for her work, including a Silver Echo Award from the Direct Marketing Association and numerous awards from the New York Film and Television Festival. Clients include: Guardian Life Insurance, American Express Financial Services, PricewaterhouseCoopers, Deloitte & Touche, the city of Minneapolis, Resource Center of the Americas, The Wilder Foundation, and Wilderness Inquiry.

Contents

Preface to the Second Edition

When the first edition of this workbook was published in 1990, many nonprofit organizations questioned whether marketing really fit with the nature and spirit of mission-driven work. In the decade that followed—as more and more nonprofits delved into marketing—worst-case fears weren't realized: the sector did not sell its soul. Instead, the *best* has happened: the sector is stronger, smarter, and growing rapidly worldwide. Today, the answer to whether marketing fits is a resounding *yes* and the burning interest is *how to realize the power of marketing for the mission.*

We stand at the beginning of an era to rival the Renaissance. The borderless economy, based on instantaneous global access to information, goods, and services, is just one manifestation of this new knowledge era. Writing in the year 2001, one can only guess how long the U.S. economic boom and phenomenal opportunity for nonprofit causes will go on, but one needn't have a crystal ball to predict the transformational impact of changing demographics, networked society, and technologies just being created.

In this context, a bit about the second edition:

New century, same message: Nonprofits that learn and apply the marketing discipline are apt to flourish.

New content, same simplicity: Readers told us, "Don't lose the simple straightforward process of the original edition." We haven't. Yet internet examples and "web wisdom" are added throughout, as are new marketing insights and expanded references.

More than 35,000 copies of *Marketing Workbooks Volumes I* and *II* have sold worldwide. We are most grateful to you, our customers, for joining in the work and for finding the value of these guides.

Gary J. Stern
Minneapolis
February 2001

Demystifying Marketing

PART I

There's a Spirit to It

EFFECTIVE marketing makes things happen—funding increases, an empty hall becomes a human rainbow, on-line volunteers win a crucial advocacy fight, essential needs are more powerfully met. There's a spirit to marketing that says "anything is possible!" and inspires a *marketing mind* that is always on the lookout for ways to bring a vision into reality.

In some marketing meetings, the air is electric. Ideas come fast, connections happen, people see something come to life. It's like that old Judy Garland and Mickey Rooney movie where one of the kids says, "Let's do a show!" And another pipes up, "My uncle has a barn!" Then another, "I know where we can get some old costumes!" And in the next scene, swarms of kids, and carpenters, and the mayor and police chief are all dashing about helping put up the show, which ends up on Broadway.

(It's not often so simple, of course, but that's the idea.)

Once suspect and forbidding, marketing is now part of the everyday world of many nonprofits. This workbook is meant to welcome you to that world, guide you through it, and help improve your marketing efforts in a friendly and informative way. Marketing can help you

Effective marketing makes things happen—funding increases, an empty hall becomes a human rainbow, on-line volunteers win a crucial advocacy battle, essential needs are more powerfully met.

- Define your niche and be sure you have the right services that deliver what people value

- Develop clear and measurable goals with genuine buy-in across the organization

- Reach the audiences you want with a message that motivates people to respond

- Decide what you want, go after it, and become a more prosperous organization with increased resources to carry out your mission

- Stand out from the crowd and attract the kind of attention, support, and enthusiasm you need and deserve

- Have a greater impact in your community and beyond

Marketing doesn't have to be confusing and complex. This workbook provides a basic discipline that any organization can learn and use. Once you've got it down, you will have a valuable tool, and perhaps a new perspective, that will prove beneficial time and again.

But some nonprofits remain skeptical. Isn't marketing about selling consumer products? Herbert Chao Gunther is president of the internationally acclaimed Public Media Center. *The San Francisco Examiner* hails him as "perhaps the most influential advertising strategist in the nation." Claiming the high ground in an *Esquire Magazine* interview, Gunther states:

> *Advertising is perceived as the whisper in the ear that tells you you're bad, you're wrong, you're different unless you buy something. Folks who are working for social change need to learn to use the media to turn that message around and change the whisper to something like, "If you do this kind of work, you're good, you're right."* [1]

Marketing is not hucksterism. It is not devious manipulation. It is not high-pressure selling. In no way does it compromise your ethics, your cause, or your art.

In this book, you will learn about marketing as a creative enterprise undertaken with a caring spirit. Marketing is necessary to help nonprofits promote their values, accomplish the mission, and develop increased resources and responses to address a range of compelling concerns. In every respect, your marketing effort can reflect the heart and soul of your work. When you are successful in your aims, the results will enliven and enrich both your organization and those you serve.

Marketing Is All about Exchanges

Marketing is an age-old practice. It involves two parties agreeing to a mutually beneficial *exchange*. Here is the definition of marketing for nonprofits:

Marketing is a process that helps you exchange something of value for something you need.

It is a *process* because it takes time to conduct research, develop marketing plans, and achieve results. The overall goal is to create *exchange relationships*—the kind we participate in as consumers all the time. We pay a fair price for something we want. We go to a free seminar or click into an on-line support group because we benefit. We volunteer and gain the deep satisfaction of doing good for others. We make these exchanges because we get something we *value*, as does the marketer on the other side.

---

[1] Herbert Chao Gunther, "The 1987 Esquire Register," *Esquire* (December 1987), page 104. For more information on the Public Media Center, visit its web site, www.publicmediacenter.org.

Examples of Four Nonprofit Exchanges

1. A mental health agency wants county social workers to make referrals to its new asset-building service for troubled families.

Mable health agency
Mental health agency

- Offers cost-effective ser-vice that improves family functioning

- Needs referrals for service

- Needs revenue

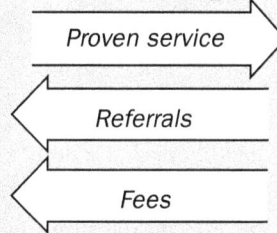

The exchange

Proven service

Referrals

Fees

County

- Values measurable improve-ment in family functioning

- Has families to refer

- Has funds

2. A neighborhood improvement association wants volunteers from an area corporation for a community paint-a-thon.

Neighborhood association

- Offers excellent community-relations opportunity

- Offers attractive activity with quick results

- Needs volunteers

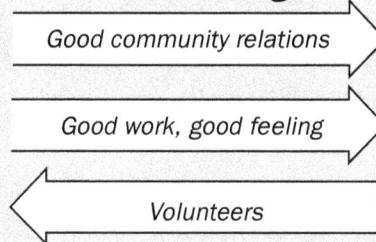

The exchange

Good community relations

Good work, good feeling

Volunteers

Corporation

- Values a community-minded image

- Values morale-building through volunteerism

- Has volunteers

3. An AIDS project wants a school board to approve implementation of its prevention curriculum.

AIDS project

- Offers sensible approach

- Needs access to schools

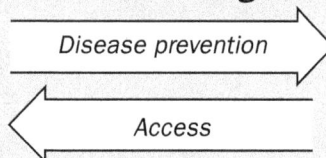

The exchange

Disease prevention

Access

School board

- Values students' health

- Has authority to implement curricula

4. A small art museum wants to expand sales of calendars and greeting cards developed from exhibitions of area artists.

Museum

- Offers "usable art" on its web site

- Needs revenue and exposure

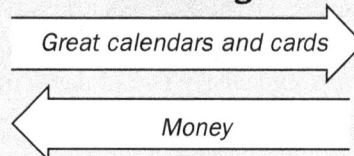

The exchange

Great calendars and cards

Money

Virtual visitors

- Value on-line purchase of calendars and cards

- Have interest and buying power

Looking back, we can see few cases in which we jumped out of bed in the morning, suddenly motivated to attend that benefit auction, join that alumni group, or map out a delivery route for Meals On Wheels. Chances are we were targeted by someone's marketing plan, possibly cultivated over time, and maybe even received a personal invitation from someone we knew. Marketing sets up these exchange relationships, and in the nonprofit world there is quite a range of them. Nonprofits make exchanges with their program participants or audience, with donors, volunteers, referral sources, friends, government, other nonprofits, small businesses and corporations—the list goes on and on.

In every successful exchange, the nonprofit offers something of value to others and receives something it needs in return. The diagram on page 5 illustrates this idea. The examples in the diagram are mutually satisfying exchanges because both parties stand to benefit; they each get something they value. Content, convenience, cost, and customer service all have to fall into place. Exchanges like this don't happen, however—except by coincidence—unless someone takes the initiative.

When *you* have something of value and want to exchange it for something you need, it's *up to you* to initiate, cultivate, and nurture exchange relationships. In other words, it's time to get into marketing.

The Marketing Process

This book introduces five marketing steps. Succeeding chapters provide guidance, suggestions, and tips for each part of the process.

The steps are:

    Step 1—set marketing goals
    Step 2—position the organization
    Step 3—conduct a marketing audit
    Step 4—develop the marketing plan
    Step 5—develop a promotion campaign

A nonprofit's sustained marketing success requires a board that believes in marketing, committed top management, and involvement of everyone in the organization. *But you can start anywhere!* Brand new programs or initiatives can be developed using the marketing planning process. In small, single-focus nonprofits, initial marketing steps may be completed for the organization as a whole. Larger multi-service groups often begin by piloting with one project, program, or division. Still others map out a comprehensive plan to become "a marketing organization," provide intensive training, and ultimately create policies and systems to sustain and reward their new practices. Wherever you start, remember that nothing builds momentum like following through and getting *results.*

Large or small, pilot project or comprehensive commitment, *it is vital that marketing plans be developed by those who will be responsible for carrying them out.* The board and top management must give direction and ensure resources to implement effective plans, but marketing edicts handed down from above are more likely to spark an unfriendly uprising than spur marketing success.

STEP 1   Set Marketing Goals

Setting goals is the first step because goals provide direction for any marketing effort. It is important early on to be as clear as possible about what you want to accomplish. Your goals tell you how you will measure success and focus your attention to achieve it.

Every marketing goal is an *action goal:* you want marketing to produce specific, measurable results for your organization. Marketing goals always define results you can count by a certain point in time: the number of people who attend a special event or sign up for a particular program, the number of volunteers recruited in a given period, the amount of money raised or new members gained from the annual campaign. A marketing goal defines how many people will "buy the product" and by when.

Set marketing goals

Sample marketing goals:

- *A junior league wants 150 volunteers by August 1 to collect and distribute school supplies for low-income students.*

- *A church wants eight couples to attend its preholiday interfaith families group.*

- *A college wants ten students to enroll in its spring semester on-line graduate course.*

- *The United Way wants fifty new leadership givers in each of its next three campaigns.*

- *A human rights coalition wants to attract one million people for a planned march on Washington.*

When first asked, "What are your marketing goals?" many groups respond with desires for their image. "We want to be better known…more widely understood and respected…more popular…seen as more activist…seen as less radical." A positive image is important—and is addressed through steps on positioning and promotion—but image must serve *action.* Yes, it's great when they know us, understand us, and like us. But the key question is, what will they *do* as a result? To move a discussion from image to action you ask, "If we had the desired image, what would people *do? What kinds of actual exchanges would we be able to count—how much of what by when?"*

Your marketing goals should strike a balance between what you ideally want to accomplish and what is possible. It's important to set your sights high *and* to respect down-to-earth limitations of time, resources, and outside factors beyond your control. The bottom line on marketing goals is furthering the organization's mission. Whether you're out to attract people, attract attention, raise funds, or raise a fuss, it's all done—and only done—if it serves to advance the cause.

Knowing what you want by when provides direction for your marketing efforts—and for use of this book. *It is necessary to work through only the marketing steps that will help you reach your particular goals.* Your numbers may feel somewhat tentative at this stage. As you learn more through subsequent steps, it is perfectly okay to revise draft goals.

STEP 2 Position the Organization

If you are unclear about what your image should be—how you want to be known by others—then completing Step 2 is important to your marketing efforts. Positioning means finding your *niche* or unique role and building your reputation. It is a long-term strategic decision that helps you define your character or *brand*: the meaning and reliable promise associated with the organization.

Positioning responds to big-picture questions about your organization or program and gives you a statement of reputation to be continually reinforced throughout your marketing efforts. As your niche becomes well known, your name will be firmly associated with the unique contribution you make ("Oh, they're the people who _____"). When people can identify your niche, they know what you offer them as well as what *they* might offer *you.* You become easily approachable by *others* seeking exchange relationships.

Position the organization

Working through positioning is critical if you're the new kid on the block, but can be equally important to established groups. If you are seen as out of step with the times, are undergoing major change, or if key audiences can't recognize what value you offer, then positioning may be key to your future success.

The positioning process in this book will help you clarify what needs and opportunities you address and identify your distinctive niche. You will develop a concise positioning statement. Then you are ready to build your reputation and gain the recognition you desire.

STEP 3   Conduct a Marketing Audit

In the first two steps you decide what you want and how you want to be seen.

In Step 3, you take stock of your marketing readiness and decide what you might change, add, or improve in order to achieve your goals.

A marketing audit is simply a short series of questions you answer to get an overall picture of where you stand right now. The questions apply equally to both "traditional" and Internet marketing. You conduct an audit using the "six Ps of marketing."[2] The six Ps provide the central framework for understanding marketing issues, diagnosing problems, and developing marketing plans. With these six words as checkpoints, you will find that marketing isn't mysterious at all.

The six Ps are:

1. **Product**—what you offer
2. **Publics**—those with whom you want to make exchanges; target audiences
3. **Price**—what you *ask for* in the exchange
4. **Place**—where the product is available
5. **Production**—the ability to meet demand and serve customers well
6. **Promotion**—what you do to convey your image and motivate people to respond

The questions for the marketing audit are based on the six Ps. Working through the questions might take as little as a few minutes at your desk or can involve intensive meetings and diving into devilish detail. When you have finished, you will know what additional information you need to make sound marketing decisions, what adjustments are necessary to correct weaknesses, and if you need to change or expand your promotional efforts. It's like going to the dentist for your annual check-up—possibly painful, but well worth it in the long run.

Conduct a marketing audit

STEP 4   Develop the Marketing Plan

Once you've done your audit, you will know where your marketing strengths and weaknesses lie, what needs to be changed, and whether you need market research. With necessary information in hand, you can develop a marketing plan that lays out how the six Ps must be aligned in order to reach your marketing goals. You can then decide on the steps necessary to implement the plan, who's going to do what, by when, and with what resources and support.

When most people say "we need a marketing plan," they often mean they want a *promotion* plan. That's because marketing as a whole is often confused with

Develop the marketing plan

---

[2] You may have seen other lists of the Ps of marketing, and you may have noticed that no two authors or instructors seem to use exactly the same words. This group of Ps is geared to the specific concerns of nonprofit organizations.

promotion—which is critical—but comes at the end of the process. Getting the first five Ps lined up comes first. That means you get information you need and make internal changes to remove roadblocks to the exchanges you want. If anything is left out of whack with any of the Ps, it throws your effort off-kilter down the line.

Having your Ps in line looks like this:

Product   What you offer is of high quality and delivers what people value.

Publics   You know your target audiences and the benefits of your product to *them.*

Price   The price is right—not too high and not too low for the value you deliver.

Place   The product is easily accessible.

Production You can effectively meet demand and serve customers well.

Promotion You convey the right image and use strong techniques that motivate people to respond.

Not every marketing plan calls for enhanced promotion. Sometimes marketing goals can be achieved through internal changes alone—adding new program elements, changing the price, putting the product on-line, improving customer service, or other adjustments to bring the first five Ps into alignment.

STEP 5   Develop a Promotion Campaign

The majority of marketing plans *do* call for promotion campaigns. They range from modest—a flyer and notice in the church bulletin—to extravagant—four-color posters, TV commercials, banner ads on portal sites, and special events featuring casts of thousands.

Whether small-scale or large, promotion campaigns include all the ways you communicate to build your image and motivate people to respond. Promotion is oriented to the *outside* world. You purposefully and deliberately call attention to yourself—often the more the better. Through promotion, you open up your doors and invite people in.

An effective promotion campaign helps to create or reinforce your desired *image* and conveys a specific *message* that tells people what you want them to do. *(Recycle! Call for more information! Visit www.ourcause.org! Exchange used needles!)* A campaign employs a mix of promotional material and techniques, each chosen for its individual usefulness as well as how it fits with the others. Thirty-one techniques are introduced and explained later in this book.

*Develop a
promotion campaign*

Living in a super-charged, multimedia world, it's easy to think marketing victories go mainly to the web-wise and televised. But none of this holds a candle to the most persuasive medium of all: *personal contact.* When you mobilize everyone associated with your organization to be enthusiastic marketing representatives, you ignite the grassroots power in your own backyard. Employing this central and highly cost-effective promotion technique is the subject of *Marketing Workbook Volume II: Mobilize People for Marketing Success.*[3]

When you have completed development of your promotion campaign, you will know

- How to define and describe your desired image
- What materials and techniques you plan to use
- How things should look and what they should say
- How you will mobilize people for marketing success
- Who will implement the campaign (including outsourcing), by when, and at what cost

Many people particularly enjoy this marketing step. You often have wonderful materials to show off, and putting the campaign into action means the real excitement is just around the corner: *results*!

Marketing's Relationship with Strategic Planning, Program Development, and Organizational Results

People frequently ask how marketing fits with other organizational efforts such as strategic planning, program development, and measuring program results. Here are the answers.

Strategic planning

Strategic planning charts the long-term direction for an organization, puts overarching goals and objectives in place, and aligns resources for desired results. The call for marketing is often an *outgrowth* of strategic planning—the need for more, better, or new exchange relationships is recognized and addressed within the plan. Some groups successfully go into marketing without a formal strategic plan in place, but if larger organizational concerns continually crop up, it is best to deal with strategic direction as soon as possible.

The Internet and other rapidly emerging technologies pose a critical issue for nearly every organization. While this workbook addresses the web from the marketing point of view, challenges and opportunities of the information age require a strategic, long-term commitment of human and financial resources for web marketing to succeed.

---

[3] Ordering information for *Marketing Workbook Volume II* and other Fieldstone Alliance publications can be found at the end of this book.

Program development

Many groups new to marketing make a common mistake when it comes to program development. Something is created and then people try to "sell it."

Instead, look at marketing as integral to your program planning and development efforts.

Nonprofits that have adopted this approach will testify to savings of time and money, greater community response, and faster achievement of their marketing goals.

Organizational results

Marketing and organizational results are intertwined. Sound marketing planning means understanding what people value and integrating key elements from start to finish. Still, marketing is most concerned with the "front end": establishing and nurturing exchange relationships. What happens *in* those relationships—whether students learn, the audience is inspired, donors feel part of the solution, volunteers know meaning in their work, or the neighborhood is revitalized—is much more than marketing. It is the total commitment of the organization to furthering the mission, to continuous

The Right Product Helps Sell Itself

The staff of a rehabilitation center is mystified. Their well-planned new concept just isn't taking off. Advance testing shows proven program results: people frustrated and deeply depressed by on-the-job injuries that forced them into long-term unemployment *do* turn their lives around through a holistic, three-week residential and outdoor adventure program. Despite an aggressive promotion campaign with e-mails, calls, and cost-savings charts, state rehabilitation counselors won't refer. With such a sound program idea, what could be wrong? They need to find out fast: the program development grant has run out and unless referrals pick up, the concept is dead.

The staff embarks on a marketing audit and decides on a series of interviews with rehab counselors to find out why they don't send their clients. The findings confirm the need for the program—counselors have plenty of people who could benefit—and also illuminate the problem. The program is "overpriced." Not in terms of dollars, but in terms of time. The counselors are simply unable to convince people who've grown so unsure of themselves to leave their home for such a lengthy

period. "They flat out refuse," says one. "These folks have lost their confidence. Packing up and going away for three weeks is just way too much to ask."

Staff worries about changing the model. It's the intensive time that enables people to gain the whole new view of themselves necessary to fight their way back. They wrestle over the question, "How do we reduce the price and keep the results?" The decision is to try lower priced "samples": a weekend try-out followed by a one-week stay with the option to extend. They're willing to bet a good taste of what they offer will build the appetite for more.

After quickly revamping the design, they convince a few of the counselors they interviewed to promote the revised approach. It works. Participants themselves are motivated and before long the new program runs at capacity. Looking back it was obvious. Program development overlooked critical knowledge of the customer, and the staff's zeal to *sell* their idea produced nothing. When marketing discipline is applied from the start, the product is more likely to sell itself.

learning, and to delivering value to customers every step along the way. Marketing results are measured in the numbers of people who buy the product. Organizational results are measured in *changed conditions* and *changed lives.*

Successful Marketing is a Sustained Effort

Marketing plans and promotion campaigns will produce great results only if they are well executed. It is important to regularly evaluate your progress and be flexible and responsive. Follow-through is paramount. As you go along, you will gain new insights, opportunity may knock, or you may run into unexpected barriers. If the marketing plan you labored over turns out to be flawed, go ahead and change it. If your intuition tells you to try a new promotional technique, see if you can work it in.

The focus at all times is achieving marketing goals. To help boost your implementation efforts, tips and rules of thumb are provided throughout this book.

Marketing success comes from solid exchange relationships. Yet people come and go, what they value changes over time, and many nonprofits face stiff competition. One of the biggest mistakes people make in marketing is thinking it's a one-shot deal. Good marketing is the exact opposite. It is a sustained effort.

Marketing becomes a powerful tool when you master its use. In the best of times it furthers growth. In the worst of times it can mean survival. At all times good marketing is like planting trees: with tending and time there is fruit.

The word to remember is *persistence* and the concept to adopt is *investment = return*. Here, nonprofits can take a valuable lesson from the for-profit world. The marketing giants invest years in developing new products, continually analyze quality, and know their promotional messages must be repeated often for customers to really take them in. We may not have for-profit marketing budgets, but as Children's Defense Fund president Marian Wright Edelman reminds us, "Don't think you have to be a big dog to make a difference. You just need to be a persistent flea."

Right now, if just starting with marketing, you might feel like a stranger in a strange land. Keeping up with marketing will be much simpler after you have completed and evaluated an initial effort. You will have a better sense of what works, more easily identify and correct problems, and be prepared to respond more quickly to opportunities that arise. Many groups go on to routinely develop annual marketing plans that build on and improve initial efforts.

Marketing becomes a powerful tool when you master its use. In the best of times it furthers growth. In the worst of times it can mean survival. At all times good marketing is like planting trees: with tending and time there is fruit.

How to Use This Book

The *Marketing Workbook* is designed to help you identify and meet *your particular needs*. You can use the book to

- Increase your overall understanding of marketing and how it can help you further the mission

- Diagnose and solve marketing problems

- Consider and integrate Internet marketing opportunities

- Develop and implement marketing plans for individual programs, services, products, or collaborative projects

- Develop and implement an organization-wide marketing plan

- Plan and implement targeted promotion campaigns

- Gain a range of new insights for increased organizational effectiveness

The workbook format is flexible. If your marketing challenges require a comprehensive approach, this book offers it. If you want to bite off only a small piece at a time, pick and choose the sections that are relevant. If changing the order of the steps makes better sense to you, feel free to do so.

To help you decide what is important for you to consider, the beginning of each step is flagged with this sign:

> **You are in the right place in this book if**

It will certainly be helpful to read through the whole book and become better acquainted with all the steps, but use the "right place" signs to decide where you want to dig in and spend your time right now.

There are worksheets for each of the five marketing steps. Completed samples are included at the end of each step. Blank worksheets are in **Appendix F**. Please feel free to make as many copies as you like and save the originals for future use.

Also, electronic versions of the worksheets may be downloaded from the publisher's web site. Use the following URL and access code (case sensitive) to obtain the worksheets:

www.FieldstoneAlliance.org/worksheets

Access code: W253mW101

To Get the Most Out of This Book...

1. Adapt the workbook to your own style.

Every nonprofit has its own way of making decisions and getting things done. You can complete marketing steps in committee, by department, with the board or a volunteer task force, or as a way to think things through alone at your desk. Adapt the workbook to your culture, your style, your interest, and your aims.

2. Involve the right people.

It is important that board members, staff, volunteers, communications professionals, and Internet experts from inside or outside the organization are a part of your marketing efforts. Remember, the best marketing plans are developed by the people who will carry them out. Be sure to *inform* everyone and follow this guide for *minimum* involvement:

- The board should, *at minimum*, be involved in decisions related to positioning.

- People in top management should, *at minimum*, be involved in approving marketing action goals and overall budgets.

- Program staff, operating volunteers, communications professionals, and Internet experts should, *at minimum*, be involved in marketing audits and decisions that affect day-to-day operations.

- Paid or volunteer communications professionals should, *at minimum*, be involved in developing promotion campaigns.

If you are putting together a special marketing task force or committee, invite representatives of your publics to contribute. The customer perspective is invaluable.

3. Keep the process alive.

Responsiveness and flexibility are crucial to success in marketing, so it is important to be open to adapting your plans. Come back to the book as often as necessary to refresh your understanding, complete sections that may not have applied earlier, and review the many implementation tips.

4. Follow through!

Make sure you have the organizational commitment and resources to follow through on your decisions about marketing. Very little is more discouraging than making earnest plans that do not lead to action.

As you get started, let this couplet by Goethe inspire you:

Whatever you can do,
or dream you can...begin it.
Boldness has genius, power,
and magic in it.

Your Marketing Effort

Set Marketing Goals

SETTING goals is Step 1 of the marketing process because goals provide direction for your overall effort. It is important right up front to be as clear as possible about what you want to accomplish. Your goals tell you how you will measure success and focus your attention in order to achieve it.

This chapter guides you through setting marketing goals. As a part of the process, you will imagine the ideal, look outside the organization to see what might be possible, and think through the resources you can realistically commit to marketing.

You are in the right place in this book if

✓ You are just getting started with marketing.

✓ You want to clarify the purpose and direction of your marketing efforts.

✓ It's time to challenge "thinking small" and imagine how much more you could achieve.

✓ You want to be specific about results and how you will measure success.

Set marketing goals

Set Marketing Goals

Setting Your Sights

Goals clarify what you want to achieve through marketing and how you will define success. This is the first step in marketing because it provides a compass for your overall effort. With that compass you continually orient your efforts in the right direction to benefit your organization.

Marketing goals: *define the specific measurable results marketing will produce.*

Your goals can cover any period of time. They may address the number of guests you want at an open house next month, set specific targets for diversity among student applicants next fall, cite numbers of donors at various levels over a five-year endowment campaign, or be the total subscriptions to an Internet newsletter you want to sell in the first two years. As you move through the marketing planning process, your goals may change. It's fine to start with your best estimates at this stage and make adjustments later.

Marketing goals clarify what you want to achieve through marketing and how you will define success.

Goal-setting worksheet

There is one worksheet for setting marketing goals, Worksheet 1. A completed sample can be found on page 28. (A blank copy is on page 153.)

Setting Marketing Goals

Marketing goals are concrete. They specify the measurable results you want for your organization or program and the time frame for those results. They are always expressed as numbers—how many tickets, how many participants, how much money, how many members, and so on. Goals cite the number of exchanges you aim to make. For some it's easiest to think of marketing goals in traditional for-profit, "unit-sales" terms: how much of our product will be bought by when.

The Internet puts many new twists on setting marketing goals. For example, if you ruled out starting a support group because there are not enough people in your service area to maintain one, creating an online group may get you to critical mass. The virtual volunteer program is another innovation. Now you can create online communities linking donors and grassroots organizations regionally.

Whether in cyberspace or on the ground, some marketing goals are determined, at least in part, by others. When you respond to a detailed request for proposals or win a contract, you usually commit to producing certain target numbers.

Your marketing goals may cover a number of categories over a period of years or be tightly focused, with the expectation of fast results. You may have many goals or only one. Each situation is unique, and your goals should correspond to what your organization or program needs.

The process of setting marketing goals opens the mind to opportunity by challenging two forms of traditional nonprofit thinking: "annualitis" and "zero-zero" budgets at the end of each year. Annualitis is the rut some people fall into because of difficult ongoing struggles for basic funding and response to the cause. When annualitis sets in, we forget how to set our sights high and begin believing that keeping even with last year or doing just a little bit better next year is the most one can hope for. When opportunity knocks, this mind-set prevents some people from answering. To combat annualitis, always take the time to *envision ideal results,* the first step when setting marketing goals.

Zero-zero budgeting is also self-limiting. Unforeseen deficits are never welcome, but some mistake fiscal responsibility for zero risk-taking and cut off the ability to make long-term investments for worthwhile returns. Because marketing is a process that involves perseverance over time, goals may take more than one year to achieve. To confront the "zero-zero" trap, set draft goals for a three-year period, look at the total investment against the total return, then budget accordingly. There are times when bigger is better, funders are impressed by a longer range plan, or the board is convinced a dip into reserves to build a world-class web site will more than pay off in the years to come. The clearest investment-return nonprofit models are in fundraising: the multiyear capital drive or direct-mail donor-acquisition campaign, for example. But investment-return thinking should be applied to every marketing effort.

At this stage in the process you set *draft* marketing goals. You will revisit goals and confirm them as part of *Step 4: Develop the Marketing Plan.* Setting draft goals requires choosing the categories in which you will set them—participation in programs, services, or events; funding; volunteer recruitment; sales of products such as books, subscriptions, or gift shop items; and possibly many other categories. Without a track record, Internet predictions are particularly difficult to make. You may wish to study current trends and talk directly with comparable organizations that are further down the road.

Most nonprofit programs or initiatives have two or more categories of marketing

"The only limits are the limits of our imagination."

Jennifer isn't sure why the executive director has insisted the whole staff set aside two days for setting marketing goals and conducting marketing audits on her program and two others. A recent graduate with a master's degree in public health, she is six months on the job with a statewide organization and thrilled to be in charge of Open Airways For Schools[4], a program that teaches elementary-school children how to manage their asthma. Things are going well; five schools have already signed on, feedback is excellent, and sixty children are being served. Respiratory therapists are volunteering to teach the sessions, and the group received an early $5,000 grant.

The goal-setting session begins well enough. Ideal results would be ten schools next year and ten each year after that. With all it takes to put the elements together and get into a school, thirty in three years would be great! But when the marketing expert facilitating the session asks a series of follow-up questions, she feels put on the spot. "Aren't there facts that argue for even better results?" the consultant begins. "How many children in this age group statewide have asthma? Aren't there hundreds of grade schools?"

Then others chime in. "How many funders have we approached? How many respiratory therapists could conceivably volunteer?" The executive director sums up, "Thirty schools would be an achievement, but I'm hearing the impact could be much greater. Think of the overall market out there. Let's come back tomorrow and talk about what's *really* possible."

Jennifer spends the last hour of the day looking up statistics, talking things through with the development director, and feeling a fair amount of anxiety about how so much more could possibly get done. She arrives the next morning willing to suspend disbelief, yet fear wells up when the group recommends that goals be set at twenty-five schools for next year, fifty more the second year, and another fifty the year after that, plus ambitious volunteer recruitment and funding goals. "We'd need to be out there with huge grant proposals," she exclaims, "and more staff! I'm really worried about how this could happen."

Her spirits rise when the executive director jumps in. "Great work! Research and feedback say it's an excellent program that really helps kids. The funding environment is strong right now and this really puts us on the map. I say let's go for it."

The details of an ambitious plan are put in place in the weeks that follow. It targets whole school districts instead of individual schools, includes promotion to respiratory therapists in major cities, lists possible funders, and has a detailed three-year budget covering all the costs. Jennifer collaborates on a six-figure grant proposal and starts to wonder if this might actually happen. She throws herself into the effort and six months later writes the following note to the marketing expert who challenged everyone in the initial session: "It's wonderful what is happening for children with asthma in our state. We've actually found a funder who put up half the three-year budget as a challenge grant and a new staff person is already hired. I can totally see it will work! This marketing process has shown me the only limits are the limits of our imagination."

---

4 Open Airways For Schools is a nationwide program of the American Lung Association.
   The case example used throughout this book is based on marketing plans of the
   American Lung Association of Arizona/New Mexico and American Lung Association
   of Texas. A special thanks goes to these groups for their contribution to this workbook!

goals. Some take into account how the Internet will contribute, some don't include Internet strategies, and some may be entirely Internet-based. To make things clear and disciplined, take one goal category at a time and work through each before starting on another.

You will answer four questions to set your marketing goals.

1. What are the ideal results we could achieve?

It's important to start here, setting your sights high. If you have to make compromises it is best to make them with the ideal—and make sure you do not succumb to "annualitis." Sometimes naming the ideal is just the touch of boldness that launches you on a course that brings it to your door.

2. What argues in favor of our ability to achieve these ideal results?

Your organization's track record is a good place to start. Is there a solid foundation to build on? Is there internal interest and enthusiasm to do more? Then look *outside* the organization to factors in the marketplace that affect you.

Have you fully tapped the prospects that may be out there? Is there high demand for what you offer? Consider the economy, trends, legislation, changing demographics, competition, and the ever-evolving possibilities of the Internet. If you are considering a highly involved or risky venture, you might need a detailed feasibility study, but if not, you simply need to bring enough knowledge to bear so you recognize what opportunities exist.

One factor to definitely consider is the size of your market and how big a share your goals represent. (This was the most important factor leading to the Open Airways For Schools program's ambitious goals—there was simply a chance to do so much more.)

3. What argues against our ability to achieve these results?

Take a second look at your track record. How good is it, really? Does the organization want this badly enough to go after it 100 percent? If you decide to do more, can you build in the funding, form a volunteer task force, free up a staff person, or go after pro bono (no charge) help? And suppose you do have some real limitations. Can you override them with sheer enthusiasm and commitment? Again, look *outside*. Are trends favorable? Do people easily "get" and respond to what you offer? How large is the market? Has interest in your offering peaked and is response in a natural decline? How stiff is the competition? Take a hard look and don't be afraid to raise difficult issues or touch on worst-case scenarios.

Set your sights high

4. **What are our realistic, achievable goals? By when?**

Having answered the first three questions, weigh the ideal results you would like to achieve against the realities of the marketplace and your internal commitment. Make sure to focus as much on opportunities as challenges—and remember, achieving ambitious goals includes increased resources, not just doing more with less. Then decide on your realistic, achievable goals and the time frame in which you believe you can reach them.

web wise

Setting Cyber Goals

Setting initial marketing goals in cyberspace can feel like jumping in with eyes closed. With little experience, who's to know? What is realistic and attainable? Does every visit to the web site count, or only those that lead to a more specific exchange? Is it success if people merely skim the surface? Or is it a matter of how many dive deep? If visitors want printed information and give their mailing address, is that an exchange? Or does it only count if they pay for it?

The key: using the web as a *promotion* tool versus offering a cyber *exchange*. (It's complex: the best web sites offer both.) **Only set net-related marketing goals if you envision actual exchanges taking place *on the net*.** And remember, measuring all aspects of visitor activity may be valuable, but at this stage focus on setting true *marketing goals*. Here is an example for an orchestra:

* *Don't* set marketing goals for the number of people who visit the site to check upcoming concert dates and availability.

* *Do* set marketing goals for the number of tickets that are actually booked online.

Although finding out when tickets are available is an important step, purchasing a ticket is an *exchange*. This is what you want to measure.

* *Don't* set marketing goals for the number of visitors who listen to a preview of an upcoming concert.

* *Do* set marketing goals for the number of listeners who tune in to a live web cast.

Surfing through the concert preview isn't the same as joining the audience. Settling in for the web cast is a true *exchange*.

And just when it might be starting to seem really clear, depending on what you decide is *actually* an exchange:

* *Do* or *don't* set marketing goals for the number of people who take self-guided music appreciation lessons, download concert program notes, or spend an evening in the composer biography section of the online library.

There are many relationship-building steps in marketing. A *marketing goal* focuses on the end point—the desired exchange.

The best sources for initial guidance are others who have plunged ahead with web marketing, combined with your own experiences surfing the web itself. Find out what you can, then proceed by cautious experimentation. The learning curve is steep. But thanks to the inherent speed and measurability of web marketing, it is also fast.

Meeting Common Goal-setting Challenges

For many people, setting marketing goals is a new process. It is a critical step in the marketing process to "get right" because your goals provide the framework for everything that follows. Once you've worked through an initial set of marketing goals, you will find repeating this step becomes simple. Here are five common challenges you may encounter and how to meet them.

- **People respond with "image goals."**

  Despite the emphasis on "how much of what by when," people frequently suggest image goals such as, "become much better known," or "gain a national reputation," or "new donors will call us because they've heard of what we accomplish."

  To meet the challenge: ask questions to focus on measurable goals, "If these things happen—if we have this image—what will we be able to count? What would people do that they aren't doing now? What would be quantifiable results and at what point in time?"

- **People respond with "process goals."**

  In this case, results are quantifiable at a particular point in time, but they measure *process* rather than outcome. You may hear, "Get a front-page story within the next three months," or "print five thousand new brochures and distribute them in May," or "redesign the web site and list keywords with all the leading search engines by January 1."

  To meet the challenge: say, "Yes, these things may be important parts of our marketing effort, but if we do them, what will be the *ultimate* outcomes we can measure? What will people do as a result of reading the front-page story? What action will they take after receiving the brochure? Once they visit our web site, what specific exchanges do we want to measure?" Keep asking, *"and then, what?"* Until you get all the way to true marketing goals.

- **People respond with percentage increases rather than actual numbers.**

  Folks are on the right track here. Percentages must simply be converted into actual numbers in order to define the necessary scope of a marketing plan. A 25 percent increase from a base of 100 is a whole different ball game than 25 percent of 5,000.

  To meet the challenge: simply do the math. Ask, "How many actual new donors… season ticket buyers…volunteer tutors…would that be?" (And don't forget to add, "by when?")

- **People respond with the number of those to be "accepted" versus the number who must "apply."**

This challenge arises when groups—such as a university admissions office or a low-income mortgage program—review applicants before they are accepted to participate. In such cases, marketing goals have two levels: the number you want to *apply* and the number you want to *enroll*. You start with the *enrollment* goal, then set the *application* goal higher—*how* high depends on the number of applicants necessary to screen in the right level of enrollment.

To meet the challenge: work backwards. Ask, "If we want a fall freshman class of five thousand, how many applicants do we need?" Or, "To give ten, ten-thousand-dollar loans to qualified first-time home buyers by December 31, how many must apply?" Or, "If we screen out some prospective volunteers once they are interviewed, how many must ask to volunteer in order to sign on twenty-five each year?"

- **People "jump the gun."**

The response runs like this, "We will increase enrollment in children's drama classes from seventy-five to one hundred fifty next year at no extra cost to us by adding culture-specific programming and teaming up with community centers who will advertise in their brochures and they already have volunteers we're sure will want to go through our teacher training and…" *Whoa!!* Time to slow down. The danger is getting committed to a whole marketing plan off the bat. An opportunity to test ideas and challenge assumptions comes in the marketing audit.

To meet the challenge: affirm all the good ideas people come up with, but only *confirm* the draft goal—enroll 150 children in drama classes next year. Note ideas and return to them during the upcoming marketing audit.

*To set your marketing goals, complete **Worksheet 1**, pages 153–157.*

It may be clear what results you want, but not so clear what you will do to achieve them. The third and fourth marketing steps, *the marketing audit* and *the marketing plan,* will help you clarify how goals can be met. When you've set particularly ambitious draft marketing goals, it's important to suspend disbelief at this stage. The audit and additional market research will either confirm your possibilities or bring you back down to earth.

WORKSHEET 1   Set Marketing Goals

In what categories will you set marketing goals?

- ☑ Participation in programs, services, or events
- ☐ Enrollment
- ☑ Volunteer recruitment
- ☑ Funding

- ☐ Membership
- ☐ Sales of tickets, books, or other items
- ☐ In-kind contributions
- ☐ Other_____

Use the following process to set your specific marketing goals.

Responses to questions 1–3 below should be brainstormed: that is, every answer is acceptable, even if they conflict.

You should make a clear decision on question 4. You may have one or more goal categories. Make copies of this worksheet and repeat these steps for *each* goal you want to set.

1. **What are the ideal results you could achieve?**

    First, define the categories of exchanges you want to make: funds, volunteers, members, in-kind contributions, and so forth, as listed in the columns at the top of this worksheet. Within each category you may have more than one goal. For example, if your goal category is funding, you might want specific results in major gifts, direct mail, and foundation grants. You might have a second goal category of in-kind contributions, with results specified in supplies, raffle prize donations, and computers.

    Now think big: if everything goes perfectly, what could the results be? (A little dreaming is fine at this point.)

Goal category	Ideal results (how much of what by when)		
Participation	**1998**	**1999**	**2000**
A. Schools	10 new/total 15 (maintain 5)	10 new/total 25 (maintain 15)	10 new/total 35 (maintain 25)
B. Children	150	250	350
C. Parents	150	250	350
D. School faculty	90	150	210
Volunteers	20 new/total 25 (retain 5)	20 new/total 40 (retain 20)	20 new/total 50 (retain 30)
Funding	$12,200	$18,000	$22,000 **Three-year total:** $52,200

2. **What argues in favor of your ability to achieve these ideal results?**

Think about factors inside the organization as well as those outside.

Inside factors working for us	*Outside* factors working for us
Participation	
1. Program has proven benefits: makes parents' and faculty's life/job easier; first-year pilots are very successful.	1. National American Lung Association core program; good marketing support.
2. Enthusiastic new staff and committed executive director.	2. Increased public awareness of asthma; school officials see effects on growing number of kids; parents will advocate for program.
3. Have good contacts with schools in two major metro areas.	3. Our state has a very high incidence rate and hundreds of elementary schools; these goals are a drop in the bucket.
4. Could use web site to update faculty, kids, and parents; could host monthly chat rooms for kids and for parents.	
Volunteers	1. School nurses and other personnel value keeping kids in school.
1. Program gives volunteers opportunity to see positive changes in kids from their efforts.	2. This volunteer population is "Internet-savvy."
2. Enthusiastic new staff and committed executive director may help attract volunteers.	3. Good response to volunteer recruitment for camp program shows market interest; medical sector is growing.
3. Could use web site to post volunteer opportunities, curriculum updates, and host monthly volunteer chat room.	
Funding	1. Incredible economy.
1. Had "easy" success finding corporate sponsor for first-year pilots.	2. Matches both corporate and foundation interests in kids' health and school performance.
2. Strong new development director.	3. No one else offers similar program.
3. Fits with strategic objective to diversify funding.	

Note: at this point in the goal-setting exercise, the marketing consultant working with Open Airways For Schools challenges the group to think much bigger. With the scope of need for the program and a promising funding environment, what if they set their sights three or even five times higher?

(continued)

3. What argues against your ability to achieve these results?

Now think about factors, inside and outside, that might hold you back.

Inside factors working against us	*Outside* factors working against us
Participation 1. Don't have enough staff, volunteers, or funds for greatly expanded program. 2. Not used to working at bigger scale, worry about maintaining quality if program grows too fast. 3. Don't have track record maintaining schools.	1. Hard to convince school officials to give release time or help with transportation if held after school. 2. Complexity of dealing with largest school districts as well as many small ones. 3. Some schools have policies against kids carrying own inhalers— necessary skill for good asthma self-management.
Volunteers 1. Staff time to recruit and retain higher number of volunteers. 2. Haven't used web site to support volunteer corps. 3. Potential "competition" for volunteers between camp and Open Airways For Schools.	1. Should have Spanish-speaking volunteers—may be difficult finding enough. 2. So much competition for volunteers. 3. May be difficult to retain volunteers —"newness" may wear off.
Funding 1. No track record yet for repeat sponsors. 2. Little experience with large, multi-year grants. 3. Development director is new.	1. Intense competition for funding. 2. Current funder interests may be passing "fad." 3. Fewer funders outside large metro areas.

4. What are your realistic, achievable goals? By when?

Try for consensus on this question.

a. Reflect on the internal and external factors, and then take a quick "gut-response" poll.

b. Discuss people's gut responses and attempt to arrive at a consensus. If you can't agree, draft low-end and high-end goals for now.

Achievable goal	By when		
Participation	**1998**	**1999**	**2000**
A. Schools	**25 new/total 30 (maintain 5)**	**50 new/total 80 (maintain 30)**	**70 new/total 150 (maintain 80)**
B. Children	**300**	**800**	**1,500 Three-year total: 2,600 children**
C. Parents	**300**	**800**	**1,500**
Volunteers	**30 new/total 35 (retain 5)**	**55 new/total 85 (retain 30)**	**65 new/total 140 (retain 75)**
Funding	**$50,000**	**$120,000**	**$120,000 Three-year total: $290,000**

Position the Organization

IF YOU are unclear what your image should be—how you want to be known—then completing Step 2 is important to your long-term marketing strategy. Positioning means finding your unique role or *niche* and building your reputation. You define who you are and how you want the organization to be recognized.

This chapter walks you through a six-step finding-your-niche process that helps you complete the phrase "We're the people who _____." Ideas and suggestions are provided to help you build your reputation.

You are in the right place in this book if

✓ Your organization needs to clarify its role or update its image.

✓ You are considering a major shift in emphasis, populations to be served, programs, methods, or style.

✓ You want to build understanding of your unique role inside the organization—among board, volunteers, and staff.

Position the organization

Position the Organization

Positioning is Finding Your Niche and Building Your Reputation

Your niche is the distinctive role you play in the marketplace. It is based on a unique ability to make an impact. Positioning flows from your mission and requires a clear sense of the organization's future direction. You first determine your niche, then build your reputation—through initial impressions, targeted messages, and delivering high-quality, results-oriented programs and services over time.

Positioning is long-term and strategic. Little is more valuable than your reputation and, once established, reputations are very difficult to change. Many groups are plagued by an outdated image that prevents people from making the right connections with who they are and what they do now. It can take years to successfully position an organization and even longer to *re*position it. Finding your niche means envisioning your unique role for the future. Building your reputation never stops.

When you have successfully positioned your organization, people recognize who you are and what you do. It makes sense to them.

Here are examples of three nonprofits that have positioned themselves well on a national scale:

- **The United Negro College Fund**—dedicated to opening doors to advanced education for African-Americans; *"A mind is a terrible thing to waste."*
- **Planned Parenthood**—frontline advocates for choice and committed providers of reproductive health services.
- **Mothers Against Drunk Driving (MADD)**—crusaders for aggressive drunken-driving policy and action and national leaders in prevention and victim assistance.

When you have successfully positioned your organization, people recognize who you are and what you do. It makes sense to them. As you build a reputation over time you will naturally deepen and expand your realm of associations. As a result, the exchange relationships you seek—and unexpected opportunities—are more likely to come your way. Effective positioning is like arriving at higher ground. It opens whole new vistas for the future.

Multilevel positioning

Figure 1

Overall organization positioning

Division or program positioning

Individual product positioning

Any organization with an essentially cohesive set of services can effectively position itself, regardless of overall organizational size. At the same time, individual divisions, programs, services, or even specific products should occupy a unique niche in their own smaller world. A visual image of multilevel positioning is provided in Figure 1 at left. The positioning process that follows is designed for the overall organization and can be adapted to individual divisions, programs, services, and products.

Positioning worksheet

There is one worksheet for positioning, Worksheet 2. It will guide you through the process of defining your niche. A completed sample copy can be found on page 46. (A blank copy is on page 159.)

A. Check In with Your Mission

The positioning statement you develop should be a direct expression of your mission—the organization's reason for being. An effective mission statement accurately defines the organization's core purpose and, in the words of Peter F. Drucker, the acknowledged father of modern management, *"It should fit on a T-shirt."*

If your mission is concise, easily understood, and provides the right sense of direction for the future, you can go on with positioning. If the mission is at all murky or there is disagreement in your group about what the mission *should* be, it is important to get this resolved. You may simply need a rewrite to bring things up to date or it may be necessary to take an in-depth look.

If there are big questions about the organization's mission and direction, then positioning has landed you at "Stop! Do not pass Go." Your marketing effort has raised questions better answered through a strategic plan.[5]

*Now go to **Section A** of **Worksheet 2,** page 159, to check in with your mission.*

---

[5] For a step-by-step guide to revisiting the mission, see the *Peter F. Drucker Foundation Self-Assessment Tool Process Guide,* (San Francisco: Jossey-Bass Publishers, 1999), pages 133–139.

Branding: Positioning by Another Name

Positioning is often discussed in the language of "building the brand." Following are definitions of key terms in the branding vocabulary.

Brand: the meaning and reliable promise associated with an organization, program, or product; its reputation.

A strong brand: uniquely identifies one organization or product from others. Frequently a well-recognized name, slogan, sign, symbol, or combination of these immediately evokes strong associations with the organization, program, or product.

Brand equity: the sum of the strong, favorable, and unique associations evoked by the organization or product and the number of customers who hold these associations.

Brand equity declines: without deliberate, continuous efforts to enhance it because of

- Competition
- Shifting markets
- Changing definitions of value

Brand equity is built: by maintaining and increasing

- Perception: "I've heard of them."
- Preference: "I have a positive association."
- Choice: "I buy from them."

Beacon House Puts a Spotlight on Mission

Beacon House was founded at the turn of the twentieth century. The original mission statement reads, *"The purpose of Beacon House is to extend the hand of God's charity to wayward girls and bring infant children into marriages otherwise deprived of this blessing."* The nonprofit provides room, board, and medical care to unwed mothers and places their babies with adoptive families. Over the years, Beacon House stopped being a "home for wayward girls" and became solely an adoption agency. By 1985 the mission read, *"To provide adoption services matching waiting children with loving families."*

The initial planning meeting for the centennial celebration touches off a controversy about how to position the agency. Looking over its history, some board members and staff are impressed by periodic changes to the mission and they begin questioning the current one.

Agency practices have changed radically in response to open adoption and other significant trends in the field. The board decides it is time to revisit the mission.

The organization decides to change the mission to reflect a vastly changed world. They identify service innovations and take advantage of the anniversary to update the organization's image. The new mission, as it enters its 100th year, reads, *"To build and sustain healthy families where adopted children flourish."*

In the case of Beacon House, something as innocent as an anniversary celebration raised fundamental questions about mission. In the process of answering them, the organization was able to envision the right niche for the future: leadership and excellence for adoption in a diverse world.

B. Look at Needs and Results

Meeting needs and getting results—both present and future—is the crux of your unique role and the driving force behind positioning. Because conditions aren't static, every successful organization's role undergoes change over time.

As you look closely at ongoing and emerging needs, opportunities for improvement and change flow naturally. You may decide to strengthen your results by adding, dropping, or improving programs. You may also consider offerings for entirely new audiences.

Years ago, in the "good cause" era, most nonprofit organizations positioned themselves as meeting compelling needs. A good cause is no longer enough. Positioning must also be based on *results*: the *changed lives* and *changed conditions* that come about through the organization's work.

You needn't address every opportunity you identify

Marketing wisdom is to make an organization's position "narrow but deep," and experts routinely counsel organizations against spreading their energies too thin. You will make the greatest impact if you are highly focused, concentrate your energies on being the absolute best at what you do, and have compelling results to show for it.

This doesn't mean you should dismiss growth opportunities or refrain from expansion. It does mean you should assess every opportunity carefully. Do you have the capacity to really make a difference? Will you have greater *results*?

*At this point, turn to **Section B** of **Worksheet 2** to record the needs you will address and results you envision. (A blank copy is on page 160.)*

C. Assess the Environment to See How You Fit In

Most nonprofits exist in an environment that is at once competitive and collaborative. It is essential to consider how you fit in. Are your offerings true standouts? Or has competition made a mess of your niche? Can you forge ahead alone and achieve strong results? Or are partnerships the best approach?

To answer these questions you will need to identify potential competitors and partners in your marketplace and learn more about them to see how you fit in. You are ready to assess the unique contribution that only you can make.

At this point, you confirm challenges to the role you want to play and decide whether you would be most effective teaming up, going it alone, or dropping out altogether. Once you know where you stand, you're ready to draft your preliminary positioning statement.

*Turn to **Section C** of **Worksheet 2,** page 47, to assess where you stand with the competition. (A blank copy is on page 161.)*

Expanded Niche Yields Better Results

A rape crisis center in a midwestern community provides intensive, long-term emotional and medical support to crime victims. Its mission is "to empower sexual assault victims to recover."

After two years of operation, the center institutes follow-up surveys. Emotional and medical recovery show good progress, but staff members note a trend in the responses that lead them to identify a "missing link." Women report their experience with the legal system as a difficult, ongoing source of stress. Staff members discuss the issue and agree that empowerment in the legal system is a critical part of the recovery process missing from their program. As there is little available elsewhere, they decide to expand their niche to include legal support services.

Depth, Breadth, and a Third-party Payer

A sheltered workshop has operated for thirty-five years and provides services to adults with severe physical and developmental disabilities. The group receives particular attention for their work site program, which brings participants into the community for supported work in nonsheltered sites.

The organization is approached to collaborate on an employment program for people with brain injuries. The opportunity involves an area hospital, noted for its inpatient rehabilitation programs, that is attached to a leading health maintenance organization. As a result, new payment sources could be put in place. The workshop wrestles with the positioning issue. Should it expand its role to serve a new participant group? Should it go after the new source of funds?

There is heated debate. On the one hand, nobody questions the need for such services, all believe the workshop could be effective, and the money is attractive.

On the other hand, the learning curve would be steep and some board members and staff have been pressing for the workshop to take a stronger advocacy role in housing, transportation, and public policy issues affecting their current participants. They believe the new venture would sap energy from these efforts.

A close vote by the board goes against getting involved in the new venture. At the same meeting, the board endorses immediate exploration of increased advocacy for the population already being served.

This could have gone either way. The group was very tempted to expand with a new population and new funds, but decided that, at least for the time being, the greater contribution would come from intensely focusing their efforts on greater results with their present clientele. They may have been entirely successful in the new endeavor but chose instead to deepen their existing niche rather than broaden it.

D. Draft Your Positioning Statement

People often ask what the difference is between mission and positioning statements. A mission statement defines the organization's purpose—its reason for being. It provides the basis for *accountability*.

A positioning statement defines the organization's uniqueness—its focused niche. It provides the basis for *reputation*.

The example of the adoption agency on page 37 shows the relationship of mission and positioning statements:

- The organization's mission is *to build and sustain nurturing families where adopted children flourish.*
- The organization wants to be known for *leadership and excellence for adoption in a diverse world.*

Positioning statements are not advertising slogans. Rather, they are straightforward and exact expressions of the organization's unique identity.

This step in the positioning process helps crystallize your thoughts into a strong positioning statement that

- Uses everyday language, avoiding technical, insider terms of your field
- Conveys the organization's character
- Is crisp and action-oriented
- Says how you want to be known

Let's look again at the three well-positioned organizations and their positioning statements from the beginning of this chapter.

- **The United Negro College Fund**—dedicated to opening doors to advanced education for African-Americans; *"A mind is a terrible thing to waste."*
- **Planned Parenthood**—frontline advocates for choice and committed providers of reproductive health services.
- **Mothers Against Drunk Driving (MADD)**—crusaders for aggressive drunken-driving policy and action and national leaders in prevention and victim assistance.

Note how each statement meets the four criteria for effective statements. They use everyday language, convey character, are crisp and action-oriented. They provide a solid basis for building reputation.

Here are three tips to help you draft your positioning statement:

1. **Summarize the conclusions you have drawn so far in the positioning process.**
   Your decisions and conclusions form the basis for your positioning statement. It's helpful to review findings before you move on.

2. **Generate lots of possibilities.**
   There are many structured methods for developing material for a positioning statement, including *brainstorming, visualization,* and *timed writing* or *drawing.* (See Appendix A for more on these idea-generating techniques.) Or, of course, you can simply sit down and do it.

3. **Beware of writing in a group.**
   Consider assigning the actual writing of the statement to one person or a small team. Writing as a group, no matter how bright and creative the members, often gives rise to "the lowest common denominator syndrome." The better role for a larger group is generating raw material, reviewing drafts, making limited suggestions, and approving the final wording.

*Now, turn to **Section D** of **Worksheet 2,** pages 163–164 and work through your draft positioning statement.*

web wise

Claiming Your Space

Just as a positioning statement is an image platform, it is also the organization's Internet platform. To build the web reputation you desire, your site must embody your positioning. Respond to the following questions to test the strength of your positioning statement from the web point of view:

1. Is everything the organization offers available on your web site, or, at minimum, can it be accessed via a web "first contact"?

2. Does your site mirror the organization's true character and depth?

3. Is the content of your site up to date? Do people get new or better information if they call or contact you in person?

4. Is your site fresh, alive, and visitor-friendly? Does it use all appropriate Internet capabilities and naturally guide people to the information or exchanges they seek?

5. If needs, results, or competition are unique to the virtual environment, do you respond as an Internet leader?

6. If people only know your organization through the web site, will their experience build the reputation you desire?

High marks on the above test means you're ready to claim your space on the Internet. If the questions leave you shaky, conducting a marketing audit and developing your plan will provide a firmer footing.

E. Test Your Positioning Statement for Support

After drafting your statement, you know what *you* believe your niche should be. You may have confirmed continuity or crafted a new approach. In either case, success in the marketplace requires support — financial, moral, political, or all three. Now it is time to confirm the viability of how you want to be known with other critical parties. It is also time to test your positioning from the Internet point of view.

To test for support, prepare a short presentation of your positioning statement and the rationale behind it, identify the six people or groups whose support is most crucial to your future success, and make an appointment to talk with them.

A list of six people or groups is a *minimum*. Go to as many potential sources of support as you feel appropriate. Potential groups for testing include the following:

- Those you serve: program participants, audience members, or those who directly represent them
- Community opinion leaders
- Funders and policymakers
- Key board members, volunteers, and staff
- Internet marketing experts

This is also a good time to seek advice. If you know people whose opinion you respect because they are wise or longtime observers of the scene, ask for their reaction too.

By testing your statement—and the logic behind it—you are already moving from finding your niche to building your reputation. As soon as you ask for others' opinions, you begin to create recognition for the unique role you intend to play. Be prepared: these discussions often lead to immediate offers of tangible support!

*Now go to **Section E** of **Worksheet 2**, page 165, for the specific steps to test your positioning statement.*

F. Refine and Clarify Your Niche

To refine and clarify your niche, revise your positioning statement, taking into account the useful feedback you have received. Some reactions may be provocative, challenging you to rethink your approach, more carefully examine risks, or raise your sights even higher. It's rare, if you feel strongly committed to what you have developed, that you will receive no support whatsoever. There are ideas that come ahead of their time and evoke outright opposition, however. It could be you've thought up a real dud, but remember that what is now the League of Women Voters got its start as a radical fringe.

Again, it can be helpful to talk through ideas and possible changes in a group, but return the statement to your writer for final revisions.

*Write your revised statement in **Section F** of **Worksheet 2**, page 166.*

Too Ready for a Fight

The board of a neighborhood development association meets in anger over the opening of a strip club near their area. They have been seen as a quiet group, more noted for rehabbing houses and community gardening than getting involved in steamy issues, but some board members are arguing for change. They work through the steps of positioning and find their "quality of neighborhood life" mission still fits. They fear the club is attracting prostitution and other crime and that no other group is in a position to battle it. With a strong sense of momentum, they describe their expanded role as "an activist force, fighting for quality of life."

A visit is arranged with the neighborhood's city council representative. Although the council member is sympathetic to the group's concerns, she advises them to "tone down the rhetoric a bit." She says the council as a whole supports quality of life efforts and that there has recently been discussion of how to better engage residents to work *with* them for change. She offers to set up an immediate meeting with law enforcement officials and suggests the group might enjoy greater support if they position themselves as interested in working cooperatively, rather than spoiling for a fight.

By testing their positioning statement, the neighborhood group learned in advance how they might modify their approach to increase support from at least one key quarter. There is skepticism as to whether they are just being "pacified," but the group decides to try "working" for quality of life before positioning themselves as a more militant force.

The Virtual Foundation: Leadership in Borderless Philanthropy for Grassroots Action on the Environment, Health, and Sustainable Development

Advanced communications technology makes it possible for a group in Nepal to apply for funds for a local reforestation project, have its request endorsed within a week by Virtual Foundation board members scattered around the world, and find a donor interested in supporting it. Operated by Ecologia, a grassroots environmental group headquartered in rural Pennsylvania, Virtual Foundation's hope is "to help accomplish what was the great promise of the Internet: that it would become a global community. A community is a place where friends help friends, neighbors help neighbors—and where people halfway around the world who don't speak our language can become our neighbors."

The foundation supports grassroots activists in Asia and eastern and central Europe who seek financing for projects endorsed by a trusted network which, in 2000, included the Baikal Center in Russia, Green Earth Volunteers in China, the Environmental Partnership for Central Europe, and the Himalayan Light Foundation in Nepal. Prospective grantees post requests on the foundation's web site (www.virtualfoundation.org). Grants ranging from $100 to $5,000 then come from high-school groups, individuals, religious congregations, small foundations, and others who access the web site (thousands each month) and search for projects that appeal to them.

According to Ecologia President Randy Kritkausky, the borderless foundation "is asking people to share their wealth. But in exchange for their donation to a project, we're helping them to develop a personal connection with the group they're donating to." Online progress reports are required of grantees. This often leads to e-mail correspondence with donors and even self-arranged international visits to project sites. People who never before gave internationally are coming back again and again.

Innovation, crystal-clear positioning, a thorough grasp of the power of the Internet, and inspired delivery add up to true leadership in borderless philanthropy. With Ecologia's blessing and endorsement, the Virtual Foundation Japan is up and running, the Czech Republic is on deck, and others are sure to follow. Different continents, same niche: borderless philanthropy for grass-roots action on the environment, health, and sustainable development.[6]

---

[6] "Virtual Foundation aims to bring international philanthropy to the masses" by Stephen G. Greene, *Chronicle of Philanthropy*, January 13, 2000.

Tips for Building Your Reputation

1. **Make sure your entire board, volunteer corps, and staff are aware of your positioning statement and understand what it means for the organization.**

   It's a good idea to reinforce this in a number of ways, such as informal conversations, meetings, memos, screen-saver messages, and in-house newsletters. Be sure to invite comments from anyone who hasn't been involved to date in the positioning process. Remember, your positioning statement not only provides the platform for the image you project, but serves as an internal tool to help make your focus and identity clear.

2. **Continue to test your positioning statement with a broader circle of people in the community.**

   There is no more powerful way to build awareness, involvement, and support than by person-to-person meetings.

3. **Make a consistent public statement.**

   Develop a boilerplate paragraph for your organization and use it in all publications and promotion. A boilerplate is a description of your organization that is a composite of your mission and positioning statements. It should also include key messages that help build the reputation you want. Here is a sample boilerplate:

   > *The Greater Regional Association of Nonprofit Theorists (GRANT) is at the crossroads of philanthropy in Texas, providing the most comprehensive and up-to-date information on philanthropic trends. GRANT's research, conferences, web site, and publications help corporations, foundations, and social entrepreneurs make the most informed giving decisions possible. Established in 1950 and awarded a Presidential Medal for Community Service in 1995, GRANT is the oldest and largest organization of its kind in the United States.*

   The reputation you want must continually be reinforced. You can't repeat your boilerplate and key messages often enough.

4. **Maintain a leadership presence.**

   Be sure people in your organization join—and seek leadership roles in—professional networks, associations, and online communities in your field. Showing up and being a leader among peers increases your visibility and brings recognition and opportunity with it.

5. **Become known by the media.**

   You are an authority in your own area of expertise. Find out who in various media covers your issues, introduce yourself, and make your organization a reliable source. And when you deserve feature coverage for your innovations or results, use your contacts, and go after it.

6. **Publish, teach, tour, and link.**

Many organizations develop specific and unique knowledge worthy of passing along. Whether it's a book, CD-ROM, conference presentation, web-cast, or community education class, publishing and teaching bring credibility, attention, and respect. In the arts, regional, national, or international touring may be a geographic positioning strategy in its own right and set the stage for a triumphal encore back home.

7. **Take a stand.**

When issues arise that affect you or those you serve, consider getting right out front with your values and your voice. Number one, it's often the right thing to do. Number two, you'll definitely be noticed.

8. **Join leadership networks.**

No matter what your specific mission or niche, it is beneficial to your organization to be well known and recognized within leadership networks—and not just those of the nonprofit world. For example, there are hundreds of organized community leadership development programs in the United States. Many are affiliated with chambers of commerce, United Ways, or foundations, and some are independent. If you've got one in your town, join up. If not, consider starting one.

9. **Form an advisory council(s).**

Aside from the extremely beneficial input and guidance you may receive, inviting consumers, experts, and other community representatives to advise you goes a good way toward establishing the profile you want. And remember, today's advisors can convene on the net from anywhere in the world.

10. **Be creative.**

A Canadian United Way successfully repositioned itself from needs-based fundraiser (think thermometer) to visionary community-builder (think dylithium crystal[7]). Breaking out of the box in any number of ways got the community's attention. The fall campaign theme was, "The future's so bright you'll have to wear shades." Volunteer campaigners swarmed through town in signature sunglasses day and night. Response went into warp.

11. *Deliver.*

The two most critical factors to building your reputation are superb customer service up and down the organization and top-notch performance that builds community and changes lives. There never has been and never will be a substitute for quality.

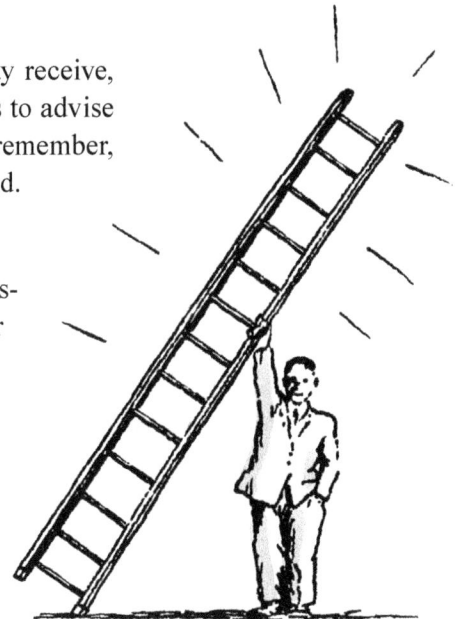

The two most critical factors are superb customer service and top-notch performance that builds community and changes lives. There never has been and never will be a substitute for quality.

There will never be a substitute for quality

[7] Dylithium crystals are the extraordinary substance that powers *Star Trek's Starship Enterprise* into warp drive.

WORKSHEET 2   Position Your Organization

SECTION A—Check in with your mission

1. Write your current mission statement here:

    To prevent lung disease and promote lung health.

    a. Is the mission clear and concise?   **Yes.**

    b. Does it address the organization's opportunities, competence, and commitment?

    **To some extent. We have differing degrees of leadership
    and depth in the major areas that impact lung health.**

    c. Does it provide the right direction for the future?   **Yes.**

2. What changes, if any, should be considered in your mission?   **None.**

SECTION B—Look at needs and results

For information to complete this section, turn first to your customers and staff. They're the best
sources you have; however, sometimes staff and customers are too close to issues and current programs to see what changes could produce even greater impact. Add some outside perspective too.

1. List the most significant ongoing or emerging needs and opportunities you will address.

    **Asthma is on the rise, especially among children in low-income communities.
    The pendulum is finally starting to swing on smoking. Settlements with tobacco
    companies and increased taxes have created unprecedented pools of potential
    funding, and public awareness is way up. Arizona used to be a clean-air mecca. There
    is renewed interest in air quality—both outdoor and indoor—especially in light of
    ongoing population booms in large metro areas. Tragically, tuberculosis (TB) is
    making a comeback, particularly in border areas. In relation to all of the above, there
    are great opportunities for making an impact through lung health research.**

2. What are your results?

    **We need to do a much better job documenting and promoting our achievements. We
    also need to develop more evaluation tools so we can continually strengthen our
    approaches. We know we've helped many individuals quit smoking, better manage
    their lung disease, and have great public recognition for being a champion of clean
    air public policy. The vision is creating a much broader and deeper impact as our
    understanding and base of resources grows. We want to see kids with asthma
    thriving, we want smoking rates to drop dramatically, we want to again be a true
    "clean air" state, and we envision indoor environments that promote lung health for
    everyone. We want to see the incidence of TB disease down to 1 in 100,000—we've
    won that battle before and we can win it again. Finally, we want recognition for the
    research accomplishments we support.**

WORKSHEET 2—Position Your Organization

SECTION C—Assess the environment to see how you fit in

1. Who else addresses issues within the scope of your mission—both on the ground and on the web?
   - **Other major public health organizations, such as the American Cancer Society, and American Heart Association, and Asthma and Allergy Foundation.**
   - **Other environmental organizations.**
   - **Government public health agencies and environmental health committees and task forces at all levels; Indian Health Services; Mexican health officials (on TB).**
   - **The Environmental Protection Agency (EPA), National Institutes of Health (NIH), and the Centers for Disease Control and Prevention (CDC).**
   - **Smoking-prevention groups and individual prevention specialists.**
   - **University research departments.**
   - **HMOs, hospitals, clinics, medical associations, individual practitioners.**
   - **School-based prevention programs and school nurses.**
   - **Businesses with clean indoor air products.**
   - **Drug companies.**
   - **Segments of the auto industry working on reduced emissions vehicles.**
   - **Alternative fuel industries.**

2. Who competes directly with you?
   - **All of the above nonprofit groups compete with us for funding and volunteers.**
   - **There is intense competition both inside and outside the public health arena for use of tobacco tax revenues.**
   - **Tobacco companies directly compete against our interests in smoking prevention and cessation.**
   - **The hospitality industry sometimes competes against us on smoke-free bar and restaurant legislation.**
   - **Some energy, development, and construction interests compete against our clean air interests; others work with us.**
   - **Some medical organizations compete in patient education, others work with us.**

3. What strengths do you bring to both collaboration and competition?

   We have a strong reputation and good performance in our public policy work, especially in clean air and tobacco control. We have extensive connections in respiratory medicine practice and research. We are a part of all major state and local coalitions in our issue areas. Our information base in lung health is strong and our national web site is taking off. We are historically the national leader in conquering TB. We have good relationships with school districts and individual schools and this is a growing area of partnership. We have offices in our two major metro areas and are expanding ties throughout the state, including with tribes. Our board, volunteers, and staff are passionate about our issues and are willing to work cooperatively. We have increased our capacity in communications and marketing.

(continued)

SECTION C—Assess the environment to see how you fit in (continued)

4. List potential partners and how you might team up with each.

> **See #1 above. We have worked with all of these groups at some level. We often share leadership roles and have joint ventures with cancer and heart. We partnered with Mobil corporation on issues research and public attitudes. We are increasingly involved with schools across our issue areas, and delivering even more is possible as we gain skill in tailoring our programs to meet the specific requirements of school partners. We're enhancing our skills in working cross-culturally. Web-based partnerships have not been extensively explored.**

There are four general ways your "fit" in the environment affects decisions on positioning. How do things look for you? Check all those that apply:

☑ There are opportunities to make a unique contribution, and we're exactly the people to do the job. Comments:

> **We are the leaders in school-based smoking-prevention and cessation and asthma education for children. We are the most trusted authority on clean air issues. There is definitely "open space" on the web in some of our areas of concentration.**

☑ It will be best to pursue results through partnerships and collaboration. Comments:

> **We play a prominent role in partnerships and collaborations on tobacco control, asthma, and clean air. We are known as a funder of lung disease research and could be known better. We could play a more significant role in TB control. We can partner with the national American Lung Association on web site development.**

☑ We need to be strongly competitive to meet needs and get results. Comments:

> **We are leaders in the fight against Big Tobacco. We could really get out in front on asthma educator certification training for health care professionals. We should more strongly stake our claim as a leader on the web.**

☑ The needs and opportunities we identified can be better addressed by others; we should back off. Comments:

> **We are most inclined to let others take the lead on issues regarding adult lung health. The Coalition for Tobacco-Free Kids is very strong as an anti-Big Tobacco voice.**

WORKSHEET 2—Position Your Organization

SECTION D—Draft your positioning statement

Your positioning statement should make it easy for people to quickly grasp who you are and what unique role you want to play.

1. To develop material for your statement, first complete the following phrases in as many ways as you can think of. (Instructions for structured ways to generate ideas are provided in Appendix A.)

   a. We're the people who…

   - **Fight lung disease, promote clean air standards, and advocate for the ill and potentially ill**
   - **Fight lung disease and promote lung health through education, research, advocacy, and community services**
   - **Lead the country in performance and cutting-edge ideas**
   - **Fight Big Tobacco and help kids protect themselves from starting smoking**
   - **Work hard to help children dealing with asthma**
   - **Improve quality of life for people who have lung disease**
   - **Help people quit smoking**
   - **Sell Christmas seals and support lung health research**
   - **Take the lead and educate the public by increasing awareness of the issues**
   - **Get attention and action from policymakers**
   - **Make air quality better**

   b. No one but no one can _____ as well as we do.

   - **Protect everyone's right to breathe easily**
   - **Educate the public on lung health**
   - **Become a real force for our mission**
   - **Influence public policy for lung health**
   - **Eliminate TB as a public health threat**
   - **Work with schools**
   - **Help kids manage their asthma**
   - **Help kids not smoke**
   - **Be known as the expert on our issues**

(continued)

WORKSHEET 2—Position Your Organization

SECTION D—Draft your positioning statement (continued)

c. We want to be seen as…

- **A leader to ensure high-quality care, education, and public policy**
- **A resource expert on lung disease and lung health**
- **A high-performance nonprofit organization with a premiere regional reputation**
- **A model multicultural organization**
- **Improving health outcomes for children with asthma and their families**
- **A respected and sought-after research partner**
- **The "air-cleaner"**
- **The people who reduced teen smoking**
- **Welcoming, friendly, great to work with**
- **A community treasure**

2. Now go back and circle the phrases that most strongly convey your niche and the reputation you want to build.

3. Based on the circled phrases in Section D, and applying the four criteria for positioning statements *(short and to the point, uses everyday language, conveys character,* and *has a sense of action),* write your draft statement here:

> **The American Lung Association of Arizona is committed to fighting lung disease, a leading cause of preventable death and disability, and promoting lung health for all Arizonans through top-quality education, advocacy, research, partnerships, and community services.**

SECTION E—Test your positioning statement for support

1. List at least five (or more) key potential sources of support with whom you will test your positioning statement.

    1. Arizona Thoracic Society chairperson

    2. Lead conveners of antismoking coalition

    3. President of Association of School Nurses

    4. Executive director of Sierra Club

    5. Executive director of new hospital foundation

    6. Recent large major giver

    7. Public relations counsel

WORKSHEET 2—Position Your Organization

SECTION E—Test your positioning statement for support (continued)

2. Make appointments with these key sources of support and, in each case, gain answers
   to these four questions:

   a. Based on your knowledge of our organization and this community, do you agree
      this is how we should be positioned?

      Yes and no.

   b. Why or why not?

      **People agree the positioning statement defines American Lung Association
      Arizona's overall niche but at the same time said it was "hard to get a handle on
      it"—too broad without making it clear what the Lung Association actually does.**

   c. How might we modify our ideas to improve them?

      **Emphasize the key areas in which the American Lung Association is deeply
      involved and actually gets results. At the same time, don't lose the overall breadth.
      Be sure to position the Lung Association as the expert source of information on all
      aspects of lung disease and lung health.**

   d. Are there other people or groups you would recommend we talk with?

      **Many helpful suggestions—people seemed to understand the positioning
      because the groups they recommended could be excellent collaborative
      partners and supporters for us.**

SECTION F—Refine and clarify your positioning statement

Write your revised positioning statement here:

   **Your expert source for stopping teen smoking, cleaner air, helping kids
   with asthma to thrive, and lung health information and research.**

*Note that with the above positioning statement, the organization's boilerplate identity statement
could use a tag line, web address, and the nationwide slogan as follows:*

   **The American Lung Association of Arizona
   Leading the fight against lung disease for all Arizonans
   www.lungusa.org
   When you can't breathe, nothing else matters.**

Conduct a Marketing Audit

IN STEP 3, you take stock. Using the six Ps of marketing as a framework, you question current and projected marketing efforts and determine what you might add, drop, continue, and improve in order to achieve your marketing goals.

The audit puts your marketing goals to a reality test. The process points out

- Positive elements you already have in place
- Additional information you need
- Changes you should make
- Benefits to promote

It is best to read the entire chapter before beginning the audit.

You are in the right place in this book if

✓ You have a marketing goal and want to know how to achieve it.

✓ You have a marketing problem but can't put your finger on what's wrong.

✓ You want to integrate use of the Internet into your marketing efforts.

✓ You are considering a promotion campaign (small-scale or large) and want to be sure it is focused and on target.

Conduct a marketing audit

Conduct a Marketing Audit

A Marketing Reality Test

A marketing audit is a reality test. You assess in detail what it might take to achieve your draft goals. Audits can be conducted with existing programs and also serve as a comprehensive framework for assessing new ones. At the conclusion of the audit, you revisit your draft goals to confirm or amend them. Then, with the knowledge gained through the audit, you go on to develop a marketing plan.

The audit helps you decide if you have the right product for the right people and what other elements of "the marketing mix" must be in place to achieve your goals. You begin aligning the *six Ps of marketing—product, publics, price, place, production,* and *promotion.* Having the *Ps* lined up means all the elements work together to produce the exchanges you want. It looks like this—whether on the web or on the ground:

PRODUCT		What you offer is of high quality and delivers what people value.
PUBLICS		You know your target audiences and the benefits of your product to *them.*
PRICE		The price is right—not too high and not too low for the value you deliver.
PLACE		The product is easily accessible.
PRODUCTION		You can effectively meet demand and serve customers well.
PROMOTION		You convey the right image and use strong techniques that motivate people to respond.

Each draft marketing goal calls for its own audit. When you have multiple goals for one program—participation, volunteers, funding, sales of materials—there will be overlap. Some groups audit against a number of goals simultaneously. Others find it simpler and more productive to address one at a time.

The actual amount of time spent on audits varies. Some people use the audit questions to help them quickly zero in on marketing "hot spots." Others conduct an in-depth assessment over a considerable length of time. Everyone who may have a role in carrying out a marketing plan should participate in audit sessions. The first audit you do usually requires the most effort; you are learning the language and concepts and naturally consider every audit question in-depth. Once you are a veteran, insights come faster.

Audits are disciplined, and the order of the questions is intentional. If discussion jumps too far ahead or veers from a focus on your marketing goals, confirm good ideas, but quickly bring the process back on course.

At the very end of this chapter, suggestions are given for putting together an audit summary or report. There, you can point out themes, overarching issues, and organization-wide implications that emerge through individual audits.

Marketing audit worksheets

There are two worksheets for the marketing audit. Worksheet 3 contains all the questions for the marketing audit and a series of *audit checkpoints* corresponding to each of the six Ps. (A blank copy of Worksheet 3 can be found on page 167.) At the audit checkpoints you stop, determine if each P is in line, and check *one or more* of the following: "OK," "Adjustment necessary," "Need information," or "Benefit to promote."

> ✓ **Checkpoint**
> ❑ OK   ❑ Need information   ❑ Adjustment necessary   ❑ Benefit to promote

❑ *OK* — *OK* means this area is in good shape. Keep things as they are.

❑ *Need information* — *Need information* means you can't fully answer the audit questions, or you need additional information to make sound decisions for the marketing plan.

❑ *Adjustment necessary* — *Adjustment necessary* means there are steps you should take to strengthen your marketing effort.

❑ *Benefit to promote* — *Benefit to promote* means this element offers a particularly attractive benefit to point out in your promotion campaign.

If you check *need information, adjustment necessary,* or *benefit to promote,* turn to Worksheet 4, page 177, to record specific questions, ideas, and concerns that will need to be addressed in your marketing plan. Completed sample copies of Worksheets 3 and 4 begin on page 75.

The *checkpoints* are a flexible tool. People who are more experienced with marketing may decide to bypass some audit questions and use the *checkpoints* alone to test their thinking, confirm how the Ps are lining up, and decide what action to take.

The Marketing Audit

The first two Ps, *product* and *publics*, are deeply interrelated. You can start in either place. When auditing an existing product, it is often best to start there. If you know your target audience and are creating a new product, start with publics. Wherever you choose to start, it's important to bounce between product and publics to make sure you've got the right match.

Product

Whether you sell it or give it away, whether it's as visible as neighborhood renewal or its province is the human heart, what your organization offers in marketing exchanges is a *product.*

What is the product?

Your product is the *something of value* to be exchanged for something you need. To market your product, you have to be able to define it so your target audiences can clearly understand what it is and what value it delivers. If people don't understand the product, find it difficult to use, or just plain don't like it, some adjustments are needed in your marketing plan.

Product

Here is the definition of a product offered to high school-age, inner-city youth by an art museum:

The product is Art Team. It is a school-year internship program providing interactive, hands-on art education and apprenticeship in the museum. Participants have a one-to-one mentor, attend an opening and closing retreat, have a weekly study group, and complete rotating internship assignments. Participants receive high school credit as well as a stipend and have the opportunity to earn wages through optional weekend work. Participants often go on to become museum employees. The elements of this product include

- *Application and screening process*
- *Mentorship guide*
- *Retreat and study group curricula*
- *Interactive assignments on a "members-only" section of the web site*
- *Internship plan and supervisor guide*
- *High school credits and a stipend*
- *Optional work program*

Is your product in line? Is it of high quality and does it deliver what people value?

To make the exchanges you want, the product must be attractive to your target audiences. And to be successful over time, it must deliver what customers value.

To answer this audit question, consider the following:

- Do you deliver value? Are you meeting the needs, wants, and aspirations of the people for whom the product is intended, your customers?
- Is there anything about the product that makes it difficult to understand or use?
- Do your customers give the product high marks?

Problems in any of these areas get in the way of satisfying existing customers—and attracting new ones.

If you find a problem with your product, it is crucial to marketing success that you make the adjustments necessary to solve it.

The Art Team program described above conducted an audit to discover why it was having difficulty filling its ranks.

After two years of experimentation and learning, the museum wants to sort out why the team is failing to achieve even the twelve-member goal it has set. It conducts a marketing audit. When looking at product questions, the team sees that the product itself is initially "hard to use" for many potential students. Team entry requirements make it impossible for the majority who apply to ever get started. Successful applicants must have high grades in school and a good attendance record. Because the screening is stiff, the "high-risk" students who may need it most can't get in. In addition, while students report they love the program once into it, the idea of the opening retreat is really intimidating.

A comment is made that grabs the audit group's attention: "It would be nice if our screening process helped screen students 'in' instead of screening them 'out.' This is a program that can benefit many kinds of kids. And why do we have to scare them to death with that retreat right at the beginning?" The team discusses the entry requirements and decides to broaden the target audience. It replaces grades and attendance with recommendations from the school, parents, church, or other youth-serving groups. An orientation session led by former participants is added to encourage new applicants and emphasize the breadth of what goes on in a museum. The team also decides to drop the initial retreat in favor of the more individualized mentor-track to get the year started. It takes but a few months to make the necessary changes and promote Art Team to the expanded audience. Team membership soars.

You may initially experience defensiveness when responding to audit questions and considering adjustments. It's hard to be objective about the need to change when you are close to your program and have strong feelings about it. This is natural, but don't let it deter you. The idea is to build on strengths, remove barriers, and discover new and better ways to attract customers and deliver value.

*Turn to **Section A** of **Worksheet 3,** page 167, to complete the product portion of the marketing audit. Write your questions, adjustments needed, and promotion notes on **Worksheet 4,** pages 177–179.*

web wise

Virtual Medium, *Real* Value

The top reasons people go to web sites are knowledge, interaction, and e-commerce—and they want value delivered in the moment.

- **Knowledge:** People need *information* and when seeking it on the web expect it to be relevant, reliable, up-to-date, extensive, and easy to download. A robust site offers any and all information related to the organization, its mission and its services, including the latest breaking news and links to sites that offer complementary depth or detail.

- **Interaction:** People who spend time in the virtual world want real relationships. Value means interaction that is engaging, informative, helpful, and, whenever possible, fun. Interaction may mean anything from a single e-mail to regular chat-room visits to ongoing membership in an online community.

- **Commerce:** If it involves money, barter, or simply providing contact information, people want one-visit satisfaction—an immediate and complete transaction.

Publics

Publics

Your product is *what* you want to exchange. Publics covers *with whom.* A *public* is a cohesive group or category of people who may find particular benefit in your product. The most desirable publics are your *target audiences*—those with the greatest capacity to make the changes you need. Individuals within those target audiences are your *customers*—the people you serve and must satisfy. Nonprofit organizations have many publics: donors, foundations, corporations, funders, referral sources, and units of government, to name a few. (Note: you may also hear the term *markets,* which means the same as publics; *market segments* are potential target audiences.*)*

Your target audiences have the capacity to give you what you need.

It is important to be as precise as possible about target audiences. The success of your marketing effort depends on pursuing exchange relationships with the *right* people, those with the capacity to give you what you need.

Who are *your* target audiences?

The problem with publics is there are so many of them! Most organizations potentially interact with a large number of groups, so how do you select target audiences, those who are most desirable? Here is the process:

1. First, brainstorm a list of every public of any importance to you. Then, choose your *target audiences* based on these criteria[8]:

   • The groups with the greatest capacity to make exchanges that will help you reach your marketing goal

   • Those with the greatest need for your product

   You may choose one, two, three, or more target audiences. It all depends on who must say "yes" in order to make the exchanges you need. A target audience can be the primary group to be served. For example, the primary group to be served by Art Team (introduced on page 58) is inner-city high school students. Important intermediaries are also target audiences. For Art Team it is public and alternative schoolteachers and counselors, parents, clergy, and community-based youth workers. A final target audience is corporate sponsors.

   Those on your brainstorm list who are not target audiences are *background publics,* groups that may be the focus of marketing efforts at another time or simply people to keep updated on what your organization is doing. An Art Team background public is school board members. They have no direct exchange regarding the program, but it's good public relations to keep board members apprised.

---

[8] A more detailed process for segmenting and prioritizing within target audiences is provided in *Marketing Workbook for Nonprofit Organizations Volume II,* pages 233–39.

Are your publics in line? Do you have the right target audiences and know the benefits that are most important to them?

2. Once you identify your target audiences, it is vital to know what each values most about your product. People are motivated to use a product because of what we perceive it will do for *us*.

   Delivering the benefits most important to your customers is crucial for products—and marketing plans—to be successful.

   Each of your target audiences may value different benefits of your product. Again, back to Art Team:

   - **Teens** value money, new experiences they enjoy and learn from, new friends, new options, and a great place to hang out.

   - **Teachers and counselors** value educational partnerships and diverse opportunities for students to achieve.

   - **Parents** value safe and constructive activities.

   - **Youth workers** value a range of partnerships and experiences that build kids' assets.

   - **Corporate sponsors** value building brand equity and engaging in cause-marketing partnerships that help kids.

   Your product is like a mirror ball. Each target audience shines a different light on it. And each sees benefits reflected back by the mirror of what *they* value.

Most nonprofit groups have an idea what their target audiences value. But, in the words of Dr. Philip Kotler, author of the pioneering work, *Strategic Marketing for Nonprofit Institutions*, "[Nonprofit organizations] often don't understand these needs from the perspective of the customers. That is the problem with many product-oriented

web wise

Who in the World?

Unlike other marketing mediums, once you're on the web, people anywhere in the world can reach you easily—and you can gather and use a great deal of information about them. This opens up

- **Opportunities** to make connections that previously were impossible, improbable, too slow, too impersonal, or too expensive.

- **New possibilities and challenges** for targeting specific audiences and individuals—as well as reaching

background publics. Just like off-line marketing, successful targeting means understanding and delivering the benefits important to each customer.

- **Policy decisions** on what information you will gather about your visitors and how you will use it.

- **Practical decisions** on what value you will deliver to people who contact you from the outer reaches.

The Seven Faces of Philanthropy

Target audiences are often described by common *demographic* characteristics. These may include age, gender, race, socioeconomic status, sexual orientation, profession, place of residence or work, and other characteristics. Taken together, these factors define an audience.

A different slant is *psychographic* characteristics. People cluster into audiences depending on what motivates them versus more obvious aspects of who they are. In their outstanding book, *The Seven Faces of Philanthropy,* Russ Prince and Karen File segment major donors into seven categories.[9] Each target audience reflects a different face of philanthropy. Prince's and File's work provides a useful example of how target audiences define what they value in unique ways as well as a useful example of

how quickly things change. Since this research was published in 1994, entirely new categories of major donors have sprung up. *Venture philanthropists, social entrepreneurs,* and other new styles could well alter the list.

Both demographic and psychographic profiles are just that: profiles. Each person is really his or her own target audience of *one.* The most sophisticated marketers carefully target the whole, then customize their approach to deliver value to each individual on that individual's own terms.

Here are Prince's and File's seven categories, the percentage they represent among major donors in the research, an identifying motto for each segment, and the key benefits they value.

Communitarian   **"Makes sense. Make contacts."**   **26%**

Value being a team member, getting public acknowledgment, and contributing to the general prosperity—it's good for business.

Devout   **"God's will. I will."**   **21%**

Act on religious values, like being a pillar of the church, prefer causes within their own religious community.

Investors   **"Good cause. Good return."**   **15%**

Require private attention and public acknowledgment. Value good stewardship and a solid—though not necessarily immediate—return on their investment.

Socialites   **"Good works. Good parties."**   **11%**

Value individual attention, public recognition, and gravitate to the arts, education, and religion. May seek status or just enjoy a good time.

Repayers   **"Made possible. Make possible."**   **10%**

Don't require much personal attention, value your effectiveness with those you serve, concentrate on health care and education.

Altruists   **"Unselfish. Understood."**   **9%**

Value personal understanding and respect, including the desire to be anonymous. Pick their causes and reward commitment and results.

Dynasts   **"Family job. Family tradition."**   **8%**

Expect to be treated as professionals, require respect for their philanthropic intent, take the long view, and focus on mission and results.

---

[9] Russ Alan Prince and Karen Mara File, *The Seven Faces of Philanthropy* (San Francisco: Jossey-Bass Publishers, 1994) pages 13–16.

organizations. They think they have such a good product, they don't understand why people are not rushing to use it. There are a lot of subtleties that require interpretation and customer research."[10] Ultimately, the only real experts on what customers value are customers themselves.

Information on what motivates your customers can come from a variety of sources. Customer research may include

- Informal observation of customers

- Your own formal research: interviews, surveys, focus groups, profiles of web site visitors, and so forth (See Appendix B for suggestions on how to do market research.)

- Studies conducted by others

- Opinions of experts and others intimate with your customers

New insights into what customers value may lead to adjustments in the product to ensure it delivers the right benefits. Knowing your target audiences' priorities, how they express themselves, and what motivates them to respond will also be essential to successful promotion. We will address this point further in Step 5: Develop a Promotion Campaign.

Turn to **Section B** *of* **Worksheet 3,** *pages 168–169, to complete the publics portion of the marketing audit. Write your questions, adjustments needed, and promotion notes on* **Worksheet 4,** *pages 177–179.*

Price

Every product has its price. In order to attract customers—and get the most out of each exchange—the price should be right: not too high and not too low for the value you deliver.

To price your product correctly, first you need to identify what you are asking your customers to "pay."

There are many nonprofit products that charge no fees to participants—shelter for victims of domestic abuse, noontime concerts in a downtown park, health service for the uninsured, opportunities to volunteer, and all kinds of information on the Internet—to name just a few. Even when the product is "free" the price always includes *time.* This is the first test of price. People must immediately feel the value of the product is worth the time it takes to get it.

Price

Many nonprofit products address intimate realms of people's lives. Here, you must have *trust.* You may fail to earn it if intake processes ask too much too soon, your approach lacks cultural sensitivity, or customers find you "overpriced" in any other way.

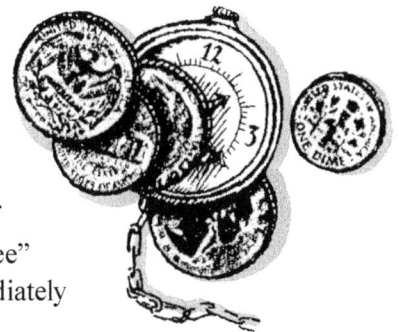

---

[10] Peter F. Drucker, *Managing the Non-Profit Organization*
(New York: HarperBusiness, 1990), pages 75–76.

And, of course, there is *money*: contributions, grants, sponsorships, contracts, ticket sales, tuition, and all manner of fees-for-service. In a highly competitive world, every dollar you ask for must deliver a value in return.

Finally, price breaks down differently in a range of exchanges, even within one program. Take a special event:

- For coverage in the newspaper, the price is column inches and a reporter's attention.
- For a celebrity to be honorary chair, the price is the celebrity's good name.
- For in-kind contributions, the price is the value of the products and the trouble it takes to donate them.
- For event volunteers, the price is their time.
- For a sponsor, the price is money.
- For the VIP reception, the price is more money.
- For whole families to turn out, the ticket price is a can of food at the door.

Is your price in line? Not too high and not too low for the value you deliver?

While much of the emphasis on getting price lined up rightfully concerns avoiding overpricing, *underpricing* can also be a mistake. Sometimes charging too little can actually devalue your product in the eyes of others while a higher price may encourage interest. Many nonprofits find that putting even a small charge on otherwise "free" services gives a sense of investment, improves attendance and, in some cases, is considered respectful of customers' dignity.

web wise

It's About Time

Misty notions that technology would liberate us all to the joys of the four-day work week have been realized in reverse. People complain of being busier than ever and when on the Internet expect instant gratification 'round the clock. In a world where every second counts, the right price means free plenty of free information and *save me time*.

Resulting rules of thumb for your web site:

- Provide a home page that delivers breaking news and serves as an enticing table of contents leading to a quick and easily navigable trip.

- Always design from the visitor's point of view.
- Give away as much information as possible—even your best stuff.
- Complete exchanges in the least possible time.
- Keep stretching for more and better commerce opportunities related to your mission.
- Be listed with all the right search engines so finding you is easy and fast.
- Provide comprehensive links to related sites.
- Be mindful of *privacy*, the hidden price all Internet customers pay.

Some products are in such great demand and are perceived to be so valuable that *high* prices should be charged. Theaters and concert halls often sell out their best and most expensive seats first. Some organizations with proven results and superb donor relations command mega-gifts. Corporate sponsors pay millions for large nonprofits' "brand equity." The finest child care centers charge rightful fees to those who can afford them (and subsidize those who can't). And some prestigious board presidencies spark intense competition for the privilege.

Clearly, "nonprofit" needn't mean low priced, however, certain offerings should be free to the general public as a matter of principle. To do otherwise undermines the mission and stature of civic institutions whose doors properly stand open to all.

Here are six points to consider in pricing a product, especially when the exchange involves money.

- What is the total cost of producing the product—including staff time, overhead, and administrative expenses?

- Do some or all of your prospective customers have the ability to pay the full cost and even allow you a "profit"?

- What is the price range in your market for comparable products?

- Is your product of such high quality and value that you can ask a top price?

- Is pricing sufficiently flexible to respect customers' dignity and include target audiences with modest ability to pay?

- Regardless of other considerations, should the product be free?

The Episodic Volunteer

The price of volunteering with nonprofit organizations underwent a sea change toward the end of the twentieth century as women continued to work outside the home in record numbers and opinion polls documented nearly everyone feeling stressed for time. Nonprofit volunteer programs struggled with this change. How could critical volunteer work get done without long-term (often demanding) commitments of time? The solution was "the episodic volunteer."

People hadn't lost their desire to volunteer. In fact, the number of Americans who volunteer increased. The episodic volunteer, highly conscious of precious time, just wanted to do it once in a while. Organized volunteerism responded with pricing that matched the customer's willingness to pay: cleaning up a stretch of creek every spring, the annual company paint-a-thon and meals-for-the-homeless days, speaking at schools during AIDS awareness week, and, in the whole-new-world category, the virtual volunteer signed on, cozy in a bathrobe. Leadership volunteering also became more flexible: boards have copresidents, key portfolios are shared by leadership teams, and years of patient "moving up" to a vice presidency is no longer the norm, replaced by in-the-moment willingness and ability to serve.

Unanticipated outcome: these episodic volunteers like their first experiences so much they sign up for lengthier installments.

Episodic volunteering is a radically changed notion of price, but the options aren't all at the low end. The most in-depth and rewarding volunteer opportunities—those perceived to have the greatest value by those who have the time—continue to command the high price they deserve.

Effective pricing means finding the right match of value and affordability. It confuses and sometimes angers your publics if you change your price too often, so thinking it through with an eye to the future is best. The only 100 percent valid test is how people actually respond. Ultimately, value—and therefore price—is in the eye of the beholder. If your price is too high, customers will stay away. If too low, you get less than you deserve.

Price can be a benefit to promote.

Low-priced and free nonprofit products are often an attractive benefit to promote. One teen-mom self-sufficiency program advertised by using a mock check with the flash headline, *$25,000 in services could be yours!* Response was tremendous and many young women said they were impressed by the real dollar value of what the program offered. Similarly, potential volunteer mentors are reminded of the worth of their time by the messages telling us, "just a few hours a month will change the life of a child." Finally, on the web, people expect immediate benefits for the time spent. Organizations with highly successful sites make sure every visit is like tasting day at the supermarket—chock-full of free samples of the great stuff you came for.

*Turn to **Section C** of **Worksheet 3**, page 170, to complete the price portion of the marketing audit. Write your questions, adjustments needed, and promotion notes on **Worksheet 4**, pages 177–179.*

Place

There is a scene in the now classic 1967 hit *The Graduate* in which a middle-aged man sidles up to the shell-shocked Dustin Hoffman during his graduation party and condenses all his worldly advice into one word, *plastics.* If worldly wisdom about marketing and *place* were to be summed up and confided in someone's ear, the secret whisper might be *bookmobile.*

Place

The genius of the bookmobile was realizing that, for many people, coming to the library was unlikely or impossible and therefore books were just going to have to come to them. With the advent of the web, the wisdom of the bookmobile seems quaint. But it was no less innovative in its time.

The value and benefit of *place,* like other elements of the marketing mix, is constantly in flux. *Place* was once a barrier to libraries being used. Today, libraries are special places where the smell of books (and often the smell of espresso) is accompanied by the *clack* of computer keyboards, and children transfixed by "story hour." In some locales, libraries are not a bad singles scene. Virtual libraries provide a *place* alternative. They may lack the sights, smells, and sounds of traditional libraries (software for this is sure to come), but their sheer accessibility makes them attractive.

Place is where exchanges occur—your organization's actual physical and virtual locations as well as people's homes, workplaces, and anywhere else you distribute your product. If people want your product, but getting it isn't convenient, you have a serious marketing barrier. Like price, place can also be a feature to promote.

Is place in line? Is the product easily accessible to your target audiences?

To answer the question, put yourself in the shoes, modems, and mailboxes of your target audiences. Getting to you should be as convenient and barrier-free as possible. If you are in a remote part of town, on the second floor with no elevator, fail to be recognized by the right search engines, or are unable to deliver the goods by 10:30 tomorrow morning, you may be considered inaccessible by your prospective customers.

Some place barriers are more subjective and include

- A location in a neighborhood perceived to be unsafe
- A location that is too public—your participants highly value their privacy
- A location that is too "ritzy"—people feel out of their element

The realities of place sometimes inspire nonprofits to shape their entire approach to service. A good example is needle exchange programs that go directly to the streets to ensure that fresh needles get to intravenous drug users. These and other frontline workers know their public isn't about to come to them, so they pick up their product and take it right to where they can do the job.

web wise

Location, Location, Location

Virtual...cyber...online...e-...it doesn't matter what qualifier goes with it, the web is a *place*. The Internet has radically redefined the concept of location and the practice of distribution. Who could have imagined vast attendance at a charity auction with no one leaving their home, no checks or cash to handle, and advance volunteers fanning out by e-mail to solicit the goods?

Every nonprofit organization must seriously consider the Internet as a commanding factor in decisions about *place*. In 1999, e-commerce was growing by 250 percent per year. *The Chronicle of Philanthropy* (January 13, 2000) predicts 25 percent of private charitable contributions will be made over the Internet by 2010.[11]

In 2000, the Ford Motor Company closed the digital divide with eligible employees worldwide via a package offer of a computer, printer, and Internet service *all for use at home* for $5 a month. Early in the new millennium, people with heart pacemakers will stand near a home sensing device, automatically transmit data, and turn on the TV for a house call from their friendly cardiologist who lives a thousand miles away.

The Internet is a *ubiquitous* medium. Occasionally crashed but never fully closed, accessible everywhere, enabling distribution of information, goods, and services at extraordinary speed and scale.

Are you ready?

[11] This prediction was one of many changes uncovered in a *Chronicle of Philanthropy* survey of 450 nonprofit executives, as reported in "Online Giving and Increased Activism," Thomas Billitteri, January 13, 2000.

Place can be a plus.

"Free parking!"

"Shakespeare under the stars!"

"Meals On Wheels!"

"On the National Register of Historic Places!"

"Webbie Award for hottest nonprofit web site!"

There may be something about your location or distribution ability that's a real plus. If you are in a particularly convenient spot, offer a special attraction, are a standout on the web, or "deliver to your door" you may have a benefit to tout.

*Turn to **Section D** of **Worksheet 3,** page 171, to complete the place portion of the marketing audit. Write your questions, adjustments needed, and promotion notes on **Worksheet 4,** pages 177–179.*

How Place Can Present a Real Marketing Problem

The Jewish Family and Children's Service of a midsized community finally realizes its dream. A capital drive raises enough money to enable it to sign a long-term lease and refurbish a central suite of offices. After many years scattered about town, its Big Brother/Big Sister program, refugee resettlement effort, elder services division, volunteer coordinators, and family counseling staff will finally be under one roof.

The new offices open with much hoopla and publicity and the energy within the agency seems to multiply tenfold. But after a few months, a disturbing trend is noted. Although a few initial intake sessions are held, virtually no new families come into the counseling program. Adding to the staff's dismay, three families abruptly terminate their therapy for no apparent reason.

A staff/board group undertakes a marketing audit and quickly decides that "place" is the issue. Other than

location, nothing has changed. They decide they need more information and, as a first step in their marketing plan, call the three families who have terminated counseling since the move.

The mini-survey provides the clue to the quandary. The first two people contacted say they found the new offices a problem, but don't say more. The mother in the third family is more blunt. "Do you think I want everyone in town to know we have problems? I felt like I was at someone's wedding reception in your waiting room!"

There was a side effect of the new location that the agency hadn't counted on. With so many people coming and going in the centralized office, counseling clients felt uncomfortably exposed. The agency developed options and ultimately decided to disperse therapists back into private offices in order to respect their customers' desire for privacy.

Production

If marketing were a religious doctrine, the longest list of common sins would appear under *production*. If you stir up demand for your product and are unable to meet it—if you're slow, late, overbooked, plagued by system crashes, out-of-stock, or lax in any aspect of customer service—you may not be forgiven, and, chances are, you'll lose customers for good. A 1987 study by Technical Assistance Research Programs documented a sobering streak in consumer behavior. Twenty-six of every twenty-seven customers who had a bad experience didn't complain, and 90 percent of them wouldn't come back either.[12]

Production

Is production in line? Can you effectively meet demand and serve customers well?

The ability to meet demand may require adequate well-trained staff or volunteers, sufficient physical space, enough inventory in stock, a one-stop-shop web site, the ability to extend the run of a hit performance, well-maintained vehicles that don't break down, good planning, and an altogether smoothly functioning organization.

This marketing question raises management and budget issues by posing a series of *what ifs*.

- *What if* our marketing effort succeeds beyond our expectations?
  Will we pull together as a team and serve everyone who responds?

- *What if* we get all four grants we've applied for? Will we be able to hire staff
  or recruit volunteers fast enough to keep our promises?

- *What if* the web site attracts an instantaneous crowd?
  Will it handle all the traffic?

- *What if* demand comes in waves? Will we be able to gear up
  and gear down?

- *What if* we have to spend more to serve more? Can the
  budget work that way or are there absolute limits?

> It's plain foolish to expect marketing to work miracles and a sin to be caught unawares when it does.

Getting production lined up means being prepared for *what ifs*—both the fat and the lean. It means adopting the kind of flexibility that allows you to continuously organize and reorganize around serving the customer. It means the ability to think big and answer when opportunity knocks. It's plain foolish to expect marketing to work miracles and a sin to be caught unawares when it does.

Serving customers well goes far beyond being able to squeeze them in the door. The lengthy waiting room experience may cause a customer to leave—for good. Voice mail over the lunch hour may mean the contribution never happens. The late fax to a prospective corporate sponsor may blow the deal. And 9-to-5 hours in a 24-hour,

---

[12] A study by Technical Assistance Research Programs cited by Tom Peters, *Thriving on Chaos* (New York: Alfred A. Knopf, Inc., 1987), page 91.

7-days-a-week world often just doesn't cut it. Customers can be extraordinarily demanding—and sometimes saying "no" is a necessity—but meeting basic standards geared to how and when customers want things to happen is critical to marketing success.

If customer service gets off on the wrong foot, that may be the first and last step in an exchange relationship. Serving customers well means consistently covering the basics and resolving problems with sensitivity and speed when they crop up. Serving customers superbly means personal attention to each individual, anticipating their interests and demands, and quickly customizing your response as much as humanly possible.

As part of the marketing plan, many organizations develop a short list of basic customer service standards, define appropriate limits on flexibility, and provide training and recognition that encourages superb customer service.

Bottom line: never make a promise you can't keep. Production heaven: delight every customer every time.

Production is a benefit to promote.

Many nonprofit services meet emergency needs and pride themselves on being able to rise to nearly any occasion. Walk-in counseling, 24-hour crisis hot lines, and the disaster-ready services of the Red Cross are examples of nonprofits whose ability to meet demand are central to what their publics value. As long as such production promises are consistently kept, they are a built-in benefit to promote.

*Turn to **Section E** of **Worksheet 3**, page 172, to complete the production portion of the marketing audit. Write your questions, adjustments needed, and promotion notes on **Worksheet 4**, pages 177–179.*

web wise

When You Build It, What if They Come?

When providing services via the web, the basic production questions apply: Will you be able to meet demand? Will you delight every visitor every time? Here are some must-haves for the web:

1. **Make sure your technology is adequate to the task.** This may mean having lots more capacity than you need for everyday use but plenty for the unexpected avalanche. The last thing you need is a "closed due to popular demand" sign out front or a systems crash just after someone has completed an online college application or planned giving profile. Which leads to the question of maintenance. If your web master is out with the flu, who will know what to do?

2. **Be ready to inter*act*.** Who will respond to all those e-mails? Who will host the 3 A.M. chat room? How will goods be shipped? Internet customer service demands are competitive and steep. If folks don't like how they get it from you, you can bet they'll go get it somewhere else.

3. **Update constantly.** First, there's site architecture and basic capabilities—for now. Web leaders innovate tirelessly, because they know today's advanced site will soon appear obsolete. And old news *is* old news. Strong production means frequent content updates, in some cases by the hour—or moment—in every case as soon as the news gets stale.

Promotion

Auditing the first five Ps is checking to see if your house is in order. Now it's time to look at promotion: how you invite people in. Promotion covers all the ways you reach out and communicate in order to create an image and motivate people to respond. It includes the broad categories of sales, advertising, public relations, media relations, and a long list of specific techniques, from business cards to web-brochures to marching down Main Street.

Promotion

Is promotion in line? Do you convey the right image and use strong techniques that motivate people to respond?

Image: how do you want to be known?

From marketing Step 2: Position Your Organization and the *Publics* portion of the marketing audit you have

- An overarching positioning statement for the organization
- Possible "small umbrella" positioning statements for divisions, programs, or products
- Lists of your target audiences
- The knowledge of what each target audience values

With these pieces in mind, you begin your promotion audit by asking,

- What do we want our image to be?
- Do our promotion materials and techniques reflect the reputation we want to build?
- Does the image we convey strike the right chord with our target audiences?

It is likely you will respond with "adjustment necessary" if

- You are a brand-new organization or program (You don't have an image yet!)
- Your product or publics are changing in significant ways
- Your image is outdated
- You believe people don't understand the value you deliver
- You want to maximize your opportunities by being better known
- You need to better differentiate yourself from others

Unless you are offering something completely new, you already have some kind of image. It may be clear or cloudy, accurate or inaccurate, positive or negative. Image adjustments come strongly into play when you want to increase your visibility or change how you are known.

*To audit your image, complete **Section F** of **Worksheet 3,** page 173.*

Techniques and tools: how you reach out and motivate people to respond

To audit your techniques and tools, make a list of what you have used and assess the effectiveness of each. (An annotated list of promotion techniques can be found in Appendix C.) A mistaken notion about promotion is that you continually have to take a fresh new approach. On the contrary, a promotion technique that worked once is very likely to work again. It will be helpful to pull together whatever promotional tools you currently have and critique them. Be careful not to get into debates based on individual taste. The three main points to cover are

1. Has this promotion technique or tool produced good response?
2. Does it convey the image we want?
3. Do we speak the language of the target audience and highlight the benefits our customers value?

What should you add, drop, or improve?

In assessing promotion, as well as the other Ps, you may have developed a number of new ideas worth exploring, decided some current techniques don't work, and noted effective tools that just need some sprucing up. The specifics of selecting and refining promotion tools comes in Step 5, Develop a Promotion Campaign, but for now, it is enough to make a general assessment of your current techniques and tools.

*Turn to **Section F** of **Worksheet 3, Question 2,** page 174, to complete the tools and techniques portion of the promotion audit. Note what you should add, drop, or improve in **Section F** of **Worksheet 3, Question 3,** page 175. (If you are conducting a marketing audit with a brand new program or product, you may skip Section F, Worksheet 3, and note your ideas for techniques and tools in the "add" portion of Worksheet 3, Section F, Question 3.)*

web wise

www.oursite.*everywhere*

To harness the promotion power of the Internet, follow five simple guidelines:

1. **Integrate your web address** into every non-Internet promotion tool you use, from business cards to special events. Tag your web address to the organization's name wherever it appears.

2. **Use free and cost-effective web-based promotion.** List your site with search engines, have yourself featured on partners' sites, get web public service announcements, buy banner ads, make sure related organizations' sites link to yours, stage targeted web-casts.

3. **Identify and be part of major portal sites** that draw and refer customers seeking what you offer.

4. **Encourage web-based conversation.** Attention-getting promotion is only a first step. Be as accessible as possible online for people to ask questions, get answers, and build a relationship. Keep those phone lines open, but offer as much web-based interaction as you can.

5. ***Deliver. Deliver. Deliver.*** Word-of-mouth is still the best advertising. At cyber-speed, it can truly make or break a marketing effort.

Wrapping Up the Audit

Worksheets 3 and 4 provide the basic information for your marketing plan. Based on what you have found in the audit, you will go on to gain more information, decide on changes and improvements, and develop a marketing plan designed to achieve your goals.

On occasion, a marketing audit points to a grim conclusion: the program or product just doesn't appear viable. Sleep on it, of course, but if this is your conclusion, go with it. Ending something or abandoning what seemed a great idea is not without pain, but a proper burial releases energy for the opportunities ahead.

In addition to completing worksheets, it is helpful to write a short summary paragraph that puts key audit findings in a narrative form. Audit summaries are especially useful if you have assessed more than one division, program, or product. An audit summary brings together the audit information and provides an overview that integrates both traditional and web perspectives. An audit summary should include

- Your draft marketing goals
- A brief product description
- Target audiences for each goal
- Key points regarding price, place, and production
- What you want your image to be
- Key findings regarding promotion
- When warranted, the recommendation to abandon further marketing efforts

Substance before Image

The image of a public health organization in a rapidly growing and diversifying metropolitan area is a prime concern for its board members. Pressure has been building for a promotion campaign to create much greater recognition. It's clear the organization plays a visible leadership role on its key issues, but the past approach has been mainly through aggressive advocacy and focused services. The group gets surprising information through customer research. Few individuals know about the organization's advocacy role (although those who do value it highly). Its services are appreciated, but across all target audiences people say they want *knowledge*—more, better, and faster access to useful information that will help them protect their own health.

The research is powerful enough to provoke a thorough marketing audit of the organization's information products. Honest assessment reveals the need for significant adjustments, including multilingual communications, faster and more frequent updating of the knowledge base, a totally revamped web site, and training across organizational "silos" so everyone can give informed initial responses to customers' requests.

It's clear the right image must convey *knowledge leadership* and equally clear it must be backed up by solid substance and excellent customer service if it is to ring true. The board agrees to be patient and management moves to make change. When the right substance is in place, the image campaign can begin.

Audit summaries are also useful as progress reports to people who participated in audits and to others interested in your marketing efforts such as board members, key volunteers, managers across the organization, and key outsiders such as funders and partners.

Take a pause at the end of your marketing audit for a deep breath. You've come a long way! Some compare their first audits to initial grueling sessions with a personal trainer—or like a trip to the dentist for a cleaning. Gym, dentist, marketing audits, they all put you in shape to look your best!

WORKSHEET 3   Conduct a Marketing Audit

SECTION A—Product   *What you offer*

1. What is the product?

> **Schools/community organizations:** A school or community organization–based asthma education program for children grades 3–5. Includes a kit with teaching material and program supplies.

> **Children:** Learning to better manage their asthma. Time out from regular classes for six one-hour sessions.

> **Parents:** More information for parenting children with asthma.

> **School faculty:** More information about working with kids with asthma.

> **Volunteers:** Learn and teach a one-hour, once-a-week curriculum for six weeks.

> **Funding:** Sponsorship of one or more schools.

2. Do you deliver value?

> **Yes. Very much so. We have sound research on the benefits to kids. Schools don't see it at first—they think of kids missing class—but once kids are into it and everyone can see results, the response is great. Volunteers really value working with kids and seeing how much kids get out of the experience. We're not as clear on how to get funders on board.**

3. Is there anything about the product that makes it difficult to understand or use?

> **Yes. Like in the last question, the issue is with some school decision-makers. School nurses understand right away, but administration doesn't initially see how Open Airways For Schools fits in school. Some people think it looks like a lot of work. Open Airways For Schools isn't hard to implement, but it does take a real commitment.**

4. Do your customers give the product high marks?

> **High marks all around.**

✓ *Product Checkpoint*
Is your product in line? Is it of high quality and does it deliver value?

☑ OK   ☑ Need information   ☑ Adjustment necessary   ☑ Benefit to promote

Write your questions, adjustments needed, and promotion notes on Worksheet 4.

SECTION B—Publics   *Those with whom you want to make exchanges; target audiences*

1. Brainstorm a complete list of publics based on each marketing goal.

   Children
   - **Kids in grades 3–5 with mild to severe asthma. Can be in school or part of a community organization such as Boys and Girls Club.**

   Schools/Community organizations
   - **Public schools**
   - **Urban/suburban/rural**
   - **Large and small districts**
   - **Private schools**
   - **Youth-serving organizations**
   - **Associations of school nurses, administrators, school boards, health specialists**

   Parents
   - **Parents or guardians of the kids**

   School faculty
   - **All faculty, coaches, administration, and others who interact with students**

   Volunteers
   - **School nurses**
   - **Health professionals—all disciplines related to pediatrics or respiratory medicine**
   - **Medical schools**
   - **Professional medical networks and associations**

   Funding
   - **Pharmaceutical companies**
   - **Other corporations**
   - **Small businesses**
   - **Foundations**
   - **Government**
   - **Public and private health care organizations**
   - **Individual donors**

SECTION B—Publics (continued)

2. Choose your target audiences for each product and note the benefits of the product they value most.

Target Audiences	Benefits
Children Kids in grades 3–5 with mild to severe asthma. Can be in school or part of a community organization such as Boys and Girls Club.	- Fun. - Get out of class. - Learn how to manage asthma better so they have fewer episodes. - Kids make new friends and feel better about themselves. - Get better grades.
Schools/community organizations - Public schools primarily, with emphasis on large urban districts and areas with highest incidence of asthma. - Private schools and youth-serving organizations are not our primary target. - Administrators, school boards, health specialists.	- Improve school performance. Healthier kids who can participate more fully in activities. - Associations are important access points. - Leadership in bringing important asthma programs into schools.
Parents Parents or guardians of the kids—through school or community organization contact.	- Kids who manage their asthma better. - Fewer family disruptions (trips to emergency room), fewer lost work days.
School faculty All faculty, coaches, administration, and others who interact with students.	- Learn how to work with kids with asthma.
Volunteers - School nurses, health professionals—disciplines related to pediatrics or respiratory medicine - Medical schools - Professional medical networks and associations	- Rewarding experience without huge ongoing commitment. - Chance for medical students to get practical experience. - Chance for medical profession to "give back"— good community relations.
Funding - Pharmaceutical companies - Other corporations - Foundations - Public and private health care organizations	- Ability to connect at local level—good community relations. - Funding that shows real results. Reduce health care costs.

(continued)

SECTION B—Publics (continued)

Target Audiences	Benefits
__Individual donors__	**Make a difference in the lives of kids. Support ALA—well known and respected organization.**

✓ *Publics Checkpoint*
Are your publics in line? Do you have the right target audiences and know the benefits most important to them?

☑ OK   ☑ Need information   ☐ Adjustment necessary   ☑ Benefit to promote

Write your questions, adjustments needed, and promotion notes on Worksheet 4.

SECTION C—Price   *What you ask for in the exchange*

1. What are you asking for? Dollars and cents or something else?

   - **Funders support Open Airways For Schools so there is no direct cost to schools or community organizations. Funding levels so far have been modest. Our largest grant was $1,500.**

   - **Open Airways takes a strong commitment from schools. There is quite a bit of time spent at the "front end" to implement the program. After that, maintenance is not time-consuming.**

   - **Parents, faculty, and volunteers—we ask time and attention.**

   - **Kids need to give their attention and best efforts.**

2. How much do you charge?

   We don't exactly "charge." We have an overall cost for the program and raise funds to cover it. We haven't broken out all the specific costs associated with the program nor have we included all staff time and associated overhead in the budget.

   We haven't quantified how much time it takes for schools to implement, but we know we could streamline the process.

   Volunteers are asked for a full day of training and then to commit to at least one six-week session per year. May need to ask volunteers for additional time to stay up-to-date.

SECTION C—Price (continued)

3. Could your customers—or at least some of them—pay more?

> **There certainly are funders who can give much bigger grants. Some schools could put more into it. We are seeing the program costs more than we have realized. We'll need to push for bigger, stronger commitments from everyone who becomes a "partner" in the program.**

✓ *Price Checkpoint*
Is your price in line? Not too high and not too low for the value you deliver?

☐ OK   ☑ Need information   ☑ Adjustment necessary   ☐ Benefit to promote

Write your questions, adjustments needed, and promotion notes on Worksheet 4.

SECTION D—Place   *Where the product is available*

1. Do people come to you or do you deliver the product to where they are?

> **We deliver directly in schools. We also want to deliver to community organizations' sites. Volunteers usually come to a central place for training. Additional information for all participants is available on the American Lung Association national web site.**

2. Are there any place "barriers" you should address?

> **Not really. We could have an improved and more customized web site here in Arizona that complements what National offers.**

✓ *Place Checkpoint*
Is place in line? Is the product easily accessible to your target audiences?

☑ OK   ☑ Need information   ☐ Adjustment necessary   ☑ Benefit to promote

Write your questions, adjustments needed, and promotion notes on Worksheet 4.

(continued)

SECTION E—Production   *The ability to meet demand and serve customers well*

1. Can you effectively meet demand?

   We can right now. We'll have to be very careful to manage the growth. To make sure we've got the staff and volunteers. We have to increase our fundraising efforts right away.

2. What if demand increases—or falls?

   We expect it to increase. We just have to be careful not to go too far out on a limb. All the parts have to work together, especially raising the money to expand.

3. Do you have standards and skills that delight every customer every time?

   We need much better tracking systems and internal customer databases. We have great people skills—the challenge will be keeping in close touch with so many customers as we expand. We will have to enhance volunteer management and be very thorough in our communications with donors.

   ✓ *Production Checkpoint*
   Is production in line? Can you effectively meet demand and serve customers well?

   ☐ OK   ☐ Need information   ☑ Adjustment necessary   ☐ Benefit to promote

   Write your questions, adjustments needed, and promotion notes on Worksheet 4.

SECTION F—Promotion   *What you do to convey your image and motivate people to respond*

1. Image: How you want to be known

   a. What do you want your image to be?

      We want to be seen as effective, a pleasure to work with, fun for kids, and rewarding for volunteers. We improve the lives of kids and their families.

   b. Do your promotion materials and techniques reflect the reputation you want to build?

      The national American Lung Association brochure and the Open Airways For Schools kit do. Some of our local materials look flat.

   c. Does the image you want to convey strike the right chord with your target audiences?

      Yes. It's what they've told us in program evaluations.

   ✓ *Promotion Checkpoint—Do you convey the image you want?*

   ☐ OK   ☐ Need information   ☑ Adjustment necessary   ☐ Benefit to promote

   Write your questions, adjustments needed, and promotion notes on Worksheet 4.

SECTION F—Promotion (continued)

2. What promotion techniques have you used? (See Appendix C for annotated list of techniques.) Note the effectiveness of each by placing a check in the appropriate column and add any comments you have.

Technique	Produces good response	Conveys image we want	Speaks language of target audience
Annual report	X		

Highlights valued benefits: **Highlights Open Airways For Schools results.**

Comments:

Brochures	X	X	X

Highlights valued benefits: **National brochure addresses benefits to all audiences.**

Comments:

Feature stories	X	X	X

Highlights valued benefits: **Yes.**

Comments: **We've had some coverage. Could have much more with focused media-relations effort.**

Networking	X	X	X

Highlights valued benefits: **People get excited about Open Airways For Schools.**

Comments:

Personal contact	X	X	X

Highlights valued benefits: **Lots of it needed to convey benefits to school decision-makers. Once they "get it," they're sold.**

Comments: **Most intensive and important promotion technique. The up-front decision-making and implementation process is time consuming and critical to success.**

Presentations	X		X

Highlights valued benefits: **Must be tailored to each audience.**

Comments:

(continued)

Worksheet 3—Conduct a Marketing Audit

SECTION F—Promotion (continued)

Technique	Produces good response	Conveys image we want	Speaks language of target audience
Special events	**X**	**X**	

Highlights valued benefits: **Good feelings and fun for a good cause.**

Comments:

Web site		**X**	**X**

Highlights valued benefits: **Good information and links for people who want more.**

Comments: **Our American Lung Association Arizona site needs more on Open Airways For Schools.**

Word of mouth	**X**	**X**	**X**

Highlights valued benefits: **First-person testimonials convey the real benefits people experience.**

Comments: **Everyone involved with Open Airways For Schools should be encouraged to be "ambassadors." New incentives for kids and recognition items for volunteers and schools will also help.**

3. What should you add, drop, or improve?

Add: **More informational and presentation materials, media relations, and use of the web.**

Drop: **Nothing.**

Improve: **Informational and presentation materials.**

✓ *Promotion Checkpoint*
Is promotion in line? Do you use effective techniques and tools that motivate people to respond?
☐ OK   ☐ Need information   ☑ Adjustment necessary   ☐ Benefit to promote

Write your questions, adjustments needed, and promotion notes on Worksheet 4.

WORKSHEET 4   Information and Adjustments

SECTION A—Information Needed

If you checked *need information* in any of the sections on Worksheet 3, write the specific questions you want answers to below:

1. **What school faculty will most want to learn in information sessions.**

2. **What parents will most want to learn in information sessions.**

3. **What enhancements to the Open Airways For Schools kit are needed? Especially incentives for kids.**

4. **Need testimonials from schools to counteract initial impression Open Airways For Schools is "hard to use."**

5. **Not sure how program will be maintained in a school after first year.**

6. **Need total numbers and names of state public schools, names and size of public school districts and private schools with geographic breakdown. Need district and school contact information.**

7. **Need lists and contact information for medical associations and pediatric and respiratory health care organizations, medical schools that place students for field experience.**

8. **Need lists and contacts of potential funders.**

9. **Areas in state with highest incidence of childhood asthma.**

10. **Analyze program to determine true costs. Determine a "cost per school" by dividing the total budget by the number of projected schools.**

11. **Focus donor research on large funders: $100,000 projects and up.**

12. **Survey a few medical associations, organizations, and schools. Will they give us time to make presentations and help facilitate volunteer recruitment? Will they share mailing lists?**

13. **What would it take to upgrade our local web site to offer more customized Open Airways For Schools information?**

(continued)

SECTION B—Adjustments Necessary

If you checked *adjustment necessary* in any of the sections on Worksheet 3, note the specific problems needing attention below:

1. Local results research to back up Columbia University study.

2. Need to tune up volunteer training and support.

3. Streamline the school's role as much as possible—take less school time.

4. Add additional supplies and incentives to kit.

5. Develop faculty and parent information sessions and materials.

6. Tune up our grant proposals—focus is higher end funders.

7. More staff!

8. Better systems for tracking contacts and managing volunteers.

SECTION C—Promotion Notes

If you checked *benefit to promote* in any of the sections on Worksheet 3 or have other notes on promotion that come up during the audit, elaborate below:

1. Results! Results! Results!

2. Each audience sees value in different terms. We need to promote what each one values to them.

3. How much do we do to make Open Airways For Schools easy and smooth for schools?

4. Open Airways For Schools is cost-effective. It saves health care costs, decreases family distress, and reduces lost school days.

5. Promotion needs to be geared individually to each target audience.

6. We make everything about Open Airways For Schools convenient for kids, schools, and parents.

7. We've got a great national web site for people to go to.

8. Need to add and revise information and materials.

9. Need incentive and recognition items that spur word of mouth.

10. Need a public relations and media relations plan.

11. Add information to our web site.

Develop the Marketing Plan

ONCE YOU'VE completed an audit, you know what is already in good shape, information you need, and where changes are necessary. In the marketing plan you lay out how the six Ps should be aligned in order to achieve your marketing goals.

To develop the marketing plan, you confirm or revise your goals, conduct research to decide how the Ps should line up, and make necessary adjustments. Then you develop steps for implementation. More detailed information and guidance on promotion strategy is contained in the next chapter, Develop a Promotion Campaign.

Note: some situations call for fast action and only a minimum of planning is possible. Even in such cases, before you put a marketing plan together, an abbreviated audit is strongly advised.

You are in the right place in this book if

✓ You have completed a marketing audit and are ready to put together your marketing plan.

Develop the marketing plan

Develop the Marketing Plan

A Blueprint

A marketing plan is the blueprint you intend to follow in order to achieve your goals. If you are addressing existing programs, the plan will incorporate the strengths of current efforts with needed changes and improvements. If the plan is for a brand new product, it will pull all the elements together for a successful debut. When you create your blueprint, fully integrate web and traditional marketing strategies.

At this point, you may confirm the goals you set earlier or revise them based on newly gained perspectives. You then summarize how the six Ps must work together: what product you will offer; to whom; how price, place, and production line up; and your approach to promotion. Finally, you detail the concrete steps you will take to implement the plan, including responsibilities, deadlines, and budget.

Marketing plan worksheet

There is one worksheet for the marketing plan, Worksheet 5, page 181. A completed sample copy can be found on page 93.

If you are looking at marketing for a number of programs, divisions, or individual products, it is best to complete the first two sections of Worksheet 5 for each. At that point, it will be necessary to take a whole view of the individual marketing plans the organization develops. In most cases, elements of separate plans are most effective when coordinated and there are perennial questions of priorities and resource allocation that management must resolve.

The Marketing Plan

Marketing Goals

Your goals provide the focus for the overall marketing effort and therefore belong at the top of any marketing plan. You set draft goals in marketing Step 1. Refer to these draft goals and respond to this question:

> Based on information and perspective gained since these draft goals were set, are they still right—ambitious, yet realistic and attainable? If not, how should the goals be revised?

*Now, turn to **Section A** of **Worksheet 5,** page 181, and restate the goals for your marketing plan.*

The Plan

Before drafting your plan, you may need to answer questions or finalize necessary adjustments identified in the audit (Worksheets 3 and 4). At this point you have a choice. One option is to go ahead and conduct research before starting on the marketing plan. This is recommended if the audit left you with major uncertainties about what your target audiences value, the root cause of any past marketing problems, or other significant questions. If you are developing a marketing plan for a "high-stakes" effort, such as a capital campaign or major geographic expansion, it is *always* best to confirm your audit findings with reliable research. If you believe you already have adequate information, go ahead and develop the plan right now.

If market research is your necessary next step, see Appendix B for guidance on types of market research and how to proceed.

Draft your plan

By now you know a great deal about how the six Ps should line up for an effective marketing plan. *Turn to **Section B** of **Worksheet 5,** pages 182–187, to fill in elements of the plan.*

Once a plan is in draft form, many groups find it beneficial to gain outside feedback—from other parts of the organization, a board committee, or marketing consultants. Asking others to look over the plan can raise important issues or details you have missed, provide good suggestions, and build interest and excitement for the effort.

Confirming Insights Builds Momentum for Change

A church-affiliated morning nursery school convenes a volunteer-led marketing task force to determine why the school can't meet its enrollment goals. The issue is particularly troubling as many child care centers in the area have waiting lists.

The audit raises significant questions about the viability of the current product in light of what target audiences value in child care. They believe they know what's wrong but need some solid answers. Over the next month, task force members conduct follow-up interviews with twenty people who have recently inquired about the nursery school but don't enroll. A consistent issue emerges: people like the school but are looking for a full-day program. The fact that the nursery school operates only in the morning makes it out of the question for most families.

Now that the problem is confirmed, the group can respond by changing the product to make it more in line with what they value. They also research a fair price for a full-day program, calculate increased costs versus revenue, and make sure their space in the church is available for additional hours.

Before it could draft its plan and gain support for change, the nursery school needed to confirm assumptions and gather new information through market research.

Here is the marketing plan for the church nursery school:

Goal: increase overall enrollment from forty to sixty children within eighteen months.

1. The product is:

A Monday–Friday nursery school and day-care program, open 7:30 A.M.–6:00 P.M. for children two to five years old. Half-day and full-day registration is welcome.

Comments:

Big change!

2. It is being marketed to these target audiences who value particular benefits of the product:

Target audience:	Benefit:	Comments:
Church members.	A safe, loving place for kids that emphasizes religious values.	Church members receive priority in filling available slots.
Families who live in the area surrounding the church (potential users).	A safe, loving place for kids that is convenient.	
Child-care placement and referral services.	A high-quality program they can refer to with confidence.	

3. At this price:

$75 per week half time.
$125 per week full time.

Comments:

Limited scholarships available to church members.

4. Available at this (these) location(s):

In the church building.

Comments:

Location gives feeling of confidence and security.

(continued)

5. To effectively meet demand and serve customers well, we will:

Increase paid staff and pursue greater volunteer involvement from church membership.

Comments:

New church board president has grandchild in school.

6. The major benefits to promote are:

High-quality program, low teacher-to-student ratio, reasonable price, religious values are taught, <u>new hours.</u>

Comments:

Strong interest in values education is helpful trend.

Our basic approach to promotion includes:

Continue to promote in church bulletin and web site, add studies and information on quality child care to the site, encourage word-of-mouth among families currently enrolled and within church community, develop and distribute new brochure.

Comments:

Ask parents for other ideas.

Implementation

The marketing plan may paint a picture very different from how things look right now or reflect the need for just a few minor adjustments. Implementing the plan means unrolling your blueprint and starting construction.

In Section C of Worksheet 5, page 188, you decide on implementation steps, assign responsibility, set deadlines, and confirm budgets.

1. **Gain necessary approvals.**

   In some cases those with the right authority to approve plans have been at the table all along. If not, marketing plans should gain whatever explicit endorsements are necessary to proceed. In the case of the church nursery school, the trustees of the church had final approval of the decision to expand and adjust budgets accordingly.

2. **Decide on steps.**

   In this section, you outline the major tasks that need to be accomplished to implement the plan and achieve your marketing goals. It may be helpful to refer again to **Worksheet 4** from the marketing audit. What needs to be addressed in order to make your marketing plan a reality? What needs to be *done?*

3. **Assign responsibility.**

   Determine who will be responsible for ensuring that each step in the marketing plan is accomplished. Being responsible for a step may mean putting together a task force, hiring or finding outside help, or delegating parts of the job to other appropriate volunteers or staff.

4. Set deadlines.

Before you fill in your deadlines, decide what the priorities are. Some steps may be urgent or naturally come first in line. If you are doing marketing planning for a special event or need things in place in time to open a new program or show, then deadlines are already set. Other situations are more flexible.

Most staff juggle marketing with other responsibilities. Be as realistic as possible and make commitments you can keep.

5. Confirm budgets.

Some of the steps in the plan have associated costs. Make sure those responsible know the parameters of their budgets.

*Now, complete **Section C** of **Worksheet 5,** page 188, Implementation.*

Most marketing plans call for a new or ongoing promotion campaign. Step 5 provides a helpful guide to more detailed planning.

Here are steps the church nursery school needed to take to implement its plan:

1. Get a provisional permit and file for a permanent change in licensure under state guidelines.

2. Decide the date the new hours will start.

3. Recruit staff and volunteers to cover extended hours.

4. Revise and expand curriculum.

5. Purchase or gain in-kind gifts of additional equipment and supplies.

6. Set up volunteer and staff training sessions.

7. Develop in-house flyer to announce new hours and contact families currently enrolled to determine how many will register for full day and to promote word-of-mouth.

8. Write a news article for the church bulletin and neighborhood paper.

9. Update the web site.

10. Meet with clergy and discuss how they will promote expanded services.

11. Make a brief presentation at a neighborhood association meeting.

12. Meet with and inform child-care placement and referral services.

13. Develop and distribute the new brochure.

14. Plan an all-school party for the first day the new hours are in place.

Tips for Implementing the Marketing Plan

1. Have a clear chain of command.

Take care to decide who has the responsibility and authority to make decisions. Sometimes a group consensus is necessary. Other times it needlessly holds things up. Define at the outset who will decide what.

2. Keep people updated and involved.

People strongly affected by the plan should already be involved, but make sure *everyone* in the program or organization—as well as key individuals outside— are aware of your marketing efforts. This creates additional support for the plan and often leads to helpful ideas and connections.

3. Keep communication flowing among all those implementing the plan.

If more than one person is implementing the plan, make sure everyone on the team is updated on each others' progress. Changes in scheduling and timing need to be communicated all around.

4. Be flexible and responsive.

Sometimes challenges and opportunities just aren't apparent until implementation is underway. Be open to expanded horizons and keep aiming for "production heaven," delighting every customer every time.

5. Evaluate, update, and celebrate regularly.

Be sure to regularly evaluate progress toward goals and celebrate successes all along the way. When things are working well, stay the course. If your situation changes, take time to stop, regroup, and revise the plan.

WORKSHEET 5   Develop the Marketing Plan

SECTION A—Marketing Goals

Write your marketing goals here:

Participation	1998	1999	2000
A. Schools	25 new/total 30 (maintain 5)	50 new/total 80 (maintain 30)	70 new/total 150 (maintain 80)
B. Children	300	800	1,500 **Three-year total: 2,600 children**
C. Parents	300	800	1,500
Volunteers	30 new/total 35 (retain 5)	55 new/total 85 (retain 30)	65 new/total 140 (retain 75)
Funding	$50,000	$120,000	$120,000 **Three-year total: $290,000**

SECTION B—The Plan

1. The product is:	Comments:
Open Airways For Schools kit with complete curriculum, four-color teaching aids, master handouts, and all necessary materials including incentives for kids. - Instructor training - Training manual - Open Airways For Schools instructor's kit - Information on asthma - Experience teaching the program - Parent and faculty education - Asthma management tools and resources	**Open Airways For Schools offers distinct products to distinct audiences. For the program to succeed, all products must be marketed in smooth concert with one another.** - Key components of the kit are available in English and Spanish. - Additional helpful information on asthma is available on the American Lung Association web site. - New kit components are great—especially incentives for kids.

(continued)

SECTION B—The Plan (continued)

1. The product is:	Comments:
Community partnerships: - **School public health partnership** - **Community group public health partnership** - **Volunteer, sponsorship, and funding investment opportunities**	

Note: The American Lung Association of Arizona developed a full-page breakout of each component of the Open Airways For Schools kit and all associated materials and supplies. This listing is an attachment to the plan, but it is not shown here.

2. It will be marketed to these target audiences who value particular benefits:

Target audiences (by goal category):	Benefit:	Comments:
School nurses and other decision-makers	**A. Builds a healthy school community** **B. Improves school performance**	**This is an overall positive. Student attendance and performance are both highly valued.**
Community organization decision-makers	**A. Builds a healthy community** **B. Enhanced youth participation**	**Fits others' mission**
Children with asthma ages 8-11 in the 3rd, 4th, and 5th grades who have permission from their parent or guardian to participate	**A. Greater self-acceptance and self-esteem** **B. Positive interaction with peers** **C. Enhanced asthma management skills** **D. Better grades**	**Kids enjoy the sessions!**
Parents of children with asthma	**A. More confidence and skill parenting a child with asthma** **B. Fewer work day disruptions and fewer emergency room visits** **C. A child who manages his or her asthma better**	**Important access point for medically underserved people.**

SECTION B—The Plan (continued)

Target audiences (by goal category):	Benefit:	Comments:
School faculty	A. **Fewer in-school health emergencies** B. **More confidence and skill in working with students with asthma**	**Eases stress and fears**
Volunteers: - **Community organizations** - **Individual medical professionals** - **Nursing, respiratory therapy, pharmacy, and other medical schools and associations**	A. **Fulfillment of a desire to contribute to a healthy community** B. **A fun, interesting, and rewarding volunteer experience with children** C. **New relationships and association with American Lung Association**	**People already doing it love it and bring in others.**
Funders/sponsors: - **Pharmaceutical companies** - **Foundations** - **Health care organizations** - **Corporations** - **Small businesses** - **Individual donors**	A. **Satisfaction of contributing to a healthy community** B. **Public recognition** C. **Brand-building through cause marketing**	**Real, measurable results.** **Great public relations and broad exposure.** **Direct connection to improving the life of a child.**

Note: Lengthy prospect and contact lists for each target audience are included in an attachment to the actual plan but are not shown here.

(continued)

Worksheet 5—Develop the Marketing Plan

SECTION B—The Plan (continued)

3. At this price:	Comments:
Per school: **$1,000/first year** **Maintenance: $120/per year.** **Commitment of school administration and health services to fully implement program.** **One-hour in-service for all staff.**	**Maintenance costs are an estimate. Will be tracked and adjusted with experience.**
Community organizations : **Same as schools.**	
Children: **Six class periods with resulting make-up work.**	
Volunteers: **Training time, commitment to teach at least one session per year. Session: one-hour lessons, once per week for six weeks, plus preparation and transportation time.**	**Initial training: one full day, refresher training time to be determined.**
Parents: **One two-hour evening program.** **Involvement time with their child on take-home materials.**	
Funders/sponsors: **Variable. Minimum amount for proactive fundraising: $500.** **In-kind contribution of program materials or supplies.**	**Contributors may receive recognition for contribution of money, goods, or services; in some cases may include use of corporate logos.**
Note: A detailed program budget was developed as an attachment not shown here. The total budget is reflected in the funding marketing goal.	

SECTION B—The Plan (continued)

4. Available at these locations:	Comments:
The program is delivered at the school or community group's chosen location.	**We go anywhere.**
Volunteer orientation is held at a central state location or in specific communities as necessary.	
A basic program description and extensive information on asthma is available on the American Lung Association National web site.	**Hope to provide more customized Open Airways For Schools options with state web site; however, national is excellent information source.**

5. To effectively meet demand and serve customers well, we will:	
Increase staff from 1.25 full-time equivalent first year to 2.6 by end of third year.	**Significant increase in staffing—need to ensure the funding plan is working!**
Be as flexible as possible in adapting Open Airways For Schools to each setting.	
Make sure volunteer recruitment and training keeps pace with growth in schools served.	**We'll need to do a great job keeping up with many more schools and managing an increasing number of volunteers.**
Provide strong follow-up and support with volunteers.	
Make sure all participants know of the American Lung Association web site and 1-800 number and know they can call the American Lung Association of Arizona for information and additional resources.	
Communicate well with each funding source to deliver results they value.	

(continued)

SECTION B—The Plan (continued)

6. The major benefits to promote are:	Comments:
- **Fun, easy, and effective for kids** - **Fewer missed school days** - **Better school performance and participation in activities** - **Asthma better managed—fewer family disruptions** - **Great volunteer experience that really makes a difference for kids** - **Great funding opportunity that makes for stronger kids and a healthier community** - **For some audiences, availability in Spanish**	**This is a program with proven, research-based results. It is absolutely worth the investment of money and time. School nurses, volunteers, parents, and all those close to the program really love it. And kids not only learn to manage their asthma better, they make new friends and enjoy the Open Airways For Schools sessions a lot.**

7. Our basic approach to promotion will include:

National brochure and fact sheet, public relations plan, inclusion in all appropriate American Lung Association materials and events, presentations and one-to-one meetings with school decision-makers, in-school information in a variety of formats, presentations at meetings and conferences for potential volunteers, mailings, phone follow-up, health journal advertising, proposals and presentations to funders, direct solicitation, recognition, and awards. **Attachments (not shown):** A. **Detailed expense and revenue budget inclusive of all program costs including administrative and indirect expenses.** B. **Item-by-item product description of the Open Airways For Schools Kit and program supplies with precise cost per item.** C. **Current customer and prospect lists: schools, community organizations, volunteer access groups, funding sources.**	**The materials, proposals, PR, direct mail, and presentations are all important, but one-to-one contact and follow-up will be essential.**

Section C—Implementation

Step	Responsibility	Deadline	Budget
1. Confirm individual assignments and get ready to staff up—get out there, make contacts, and follow-up!	Program director	ASAP and ongoing	1.4 new FTE salary, benefits, overhead
2. Develop and implement quarterly assessment of progress against marketing goals.	Program director	End of first quarter year one	
3. Develop PR plan; schedule, produce, and distribute all materials.	Director of communications and development	End of second quarter year one	$2,500
4. Continue to expand contacts list and implement a contacts tracking system.	Program director	End of second quarter year one	
5. Refine volunteer management systems.	Staff	End of second quarter year one	
6. Develop and implement volunteer and school recognition plan and materials.	Staff	End of third quarter year one	$1,500
7. Develop plan for website enhancements.	Director of communications and development	End of third quarter year one	$500
8. Assess maintenance activity and costs.	Program director	End of fourth quarter year one	
9. Formally assess and revise plan.	All	First quarter year two and year three	

Develop a Promotion Campaign

WHETHER small-scale or large, promotion campaigns include all the ways you communicate in order to build an image and motivate people to respond. In this step, you work with internal or external marketing communications and Internet specialists to determine the images, messages, and tools that will make up your promotion campaign.

For some organizations, the basic approach to promotion outlined in the marketing plan is sufficient to move forward. For many others, a comprehensive and detailed plan produces efficiencies of cost and time. Step 5 guides you through decisions on image, message, and choice of promotion materials and techniques.

You are in the right place in this book if

✓ Your marketing plan is new or calls for changes or additions in promotion

✓ You want to develop your image and key messages

✓ You want to consider a wide range of promotion tools

✓ You need a detailed promotion plan

Develop a promotion campaign

Develop a Promotion Campaign

Inviting People In

Everything in the marketing process is important, but for many people, promotion is the exciting part. That's natural because promotional activities *themselves* are rewarding. Producing a great new brochure, putting on an event, adding capabilities to the web site, or making an in-person call on a promising contact are tangible accomplishments. And when these activities produce desired results, it's time for celebration!

Specialized expertise is necessary for effective writing, design, use of technology, and proper consideration of an array of promotion possibilities.

In developing a promotion campaign you make final decisions on your desired image, determine your key messages, decide what materials and techniques you'll use, and then implement the plan. Marketing communications and Internet specialists play a key role in this step. They may be from inside or outside the organization, advisors or doers, pro bono or paid. Specialized expertise is necessary for effective writing, design, use of technology, and proper consideration of an array of promotion possibilities. Whether such specialists have been part of the crew all along or they're recruited now, it's time to determine what kind of expertise will be helpful and bring it on board.

Promotion campaign worksheet

Worksheet 6, page 189, will take you through the four areas of decision-making for promotion. A completed sample copy can be found on page 112.

Promotion Conveys an Image

Promotion materials and techniques are like ambassadors from your organization. An encounter with them is an encounter with you. U.S. experts disagree on exact figures but place the average number of promotional messages we're exposed to daily at somewhere between 560 and 1,800.[13] Internet studies tell us web sites lose 10 percent of visitors for every 10 seconds they spend at the web site. With such tremendous competition for attention and so little time to make an impression, your promotion

---

[13] *Star Tribune, Newspaper of the Twin Cities,* May 19, 1989.

has to convey something, convey it fast, and convey it well. It has to create an initial reaction that draws people in, that says, *This is good. This is for me.*

This first impression is created through *image* and *key messages*—the combination of words, pictures, symbols, colors, and sounds that present your organization or product and ask for a response.

Even in today's fast-paced, too-much-information world, nonprofits can be winners in the competition for attention. There is every reason for your mission to evoke passionate images and compelling messages that motivate people to respond.

Defining your desired image

An effective image makes the impression you want.

In the marketing audit, you responded to three image questions:

A. What do we want our image to be?
B. Do our promotion materials and techniques reflect the reputation we want to build?
C. Does the image we convey strike the right chord with our target audiences?

Note: when defining the desired image for a *new* organization or product, the marketing audit only addresses point A above, since you probably won't have existing promotion materials and image.

Your positioning statement is your "image platform." It is helpful to review it at this point. Then, brainstorm a list of colorful and descriptive words, phrases, metaphors, or comparisons that reflect your desired image.

Positioning Statement and Brainstorm List for an Alternative School:

Positioning statement:
Corner School is the place that nurtures kids and helps everyone in the school community succeed. We are advocates for opportunity, pathbreakers, and tirelessly *there* for our kids and their families.

Image reflectors:
- Teachers relate well to kids and families
- Vital part of education system
- Really there for people
- Cutting-edge, risk-takers, tech-savvy

- Warm atmosphere, lots of humor
- Culturally diverse
- Passionate about all kids and families succeeding
- High-quality, get results
- "A community garden"
- "A pillar of strength"
- Color: purple
- TV show: *A Day in the Life*
- Movie: *Stand and Deliver*
- Flower: wild Irish rose

Once you have your list, choose the words, phrases, metaphors, or comparisons that do the best job of reflecting your desired image. Don't worry if the top choices don't fit together perfectly or even if there seem to be contradictions. An image can be multifaceted.

*Go to **Section A** of **Worksheet 6,** page 189, to describe your desired image.*

An effective image works with *all* your target audiences. But image doesn't stand alone. It goes with key *messages* that should be developed for *each* of your target audiences.

Effective Messages Produce the Response You Want

An effective promotional message prompts your target audience to take a specific action and promises a valuable benefit if they do.

Since you are seeking different exchanges with specific target audiences, individual messages are tailored and distinct. At the same time, the overall set of messages promoting any organization or product should be in harmony. For example, if your product is an alternative school for adolescents, you will speak differently to professional referral sources, to parents, and to adolescents themselves.

No matter who you are addressing, your message should be in the everyday language *of that audience* and contain the essential information that will motivate them to respond.

In the marketing audit, you laid the groundwork for effective messages by determining what your target audiences value. To tailor a message that *gets through,* you also have to know

    A. Your target audience's everyday language
    B. Where and how they get information
    C. Examples of messages they already respond to

With clarity about what the target audience values and what gets through, you can now frame the three parts of an effective message:

    A. *Key benefits* that make the product valuable to that target audience
    B. *Top features and options* that are important to them
    C. *The specific, immediate action you want people to take*

Key benefits are what the audience most cares about. They may be immediate (coffee and doughnuts) or more long-term (a safe place to rebuild a life). A key benefit can be the absence of a barrier (no cost...no waiting...delivered to your door!). Benefits are "make or break." If they don't instantly say "value" to the target audience, the target audience says good-bye. *Limit yourself to defining three key benefits.*

Top features and options move to the next level of consideration. The target audience is saying, "I'm interested. What have you got?" You're saying, "a number of things that are important to you," which, again, may be an absence of barriers. Features are "fixed" (a totally up-to-date multimedia lab), options are "flexible" (design the training course that's right for you).

The specific, immediate action you want people to take is just that: register online anytime! Call us today! Mail back this postcard! Stop in for a visit! Be there…and bring a friend! *You may have one or multiple "calls to action."* They should include relevant contact information: phone number, www.oursite.org, and so forth.

Caution: a call to action may or may not be "asking for the exchange." Enrollments, season ticket purchases, referrals, donations, or firm agreements to volunteer may come now or, in many cases, later. The "call to action" asks prospective customers to *take the immediate next step.* Once they do, *you* take it from there.

The key to getting action is the *promise of a benefit.* David Ogilvy is the founder of Ogilvy and Mather, a legendary international advertising agency. In his 1983 book, *Ogilvy on Advertising,* he writes:

> *Advertising which promises no benefit to the consumer does not sell, yet the majority of campaigns contain no promise whatever. (That is the most important sentence in this book. Read it again.)* Starch** reported that advertisements with headlines that promise a benefit are read by an average of four times more people than advertisements that don't.[14]*

>   * *Ogilvy's emphasis.*
> ** *"Starch" refers to the Starch Readership Service, an organization that provides factor analyses on advertising.*

Determining key benefits, top features or options, and the call to action is not "writing the brochure" (although it may come close). Your focus right now is the *substance* of your message. A designated copywriter should absorb it all, develop initial drafts, get feedback, and do the polishing.

A sample brochure for the Open Airways For Schools case study can be found on pages 118–119. It targets school and community decision-makers. Here are the positioning statement and draft key messages for Open Airways For Schools:

Program positioning statement:

Open Airways For Schools is the only nationally recognized education program delivering proven beneficial asthma management results to children, grades 3–5, in school and community-based settings.

- *Open Airways For Schools is fun, easy, and most important, proven effective!*

---

[14] David Ogilvy, *Ogilvy on Advertising* (New York: Crown Publishers Inc., 1983) p. 160.

- *Open Airways For Schools empowers 8–11 year old children, their parents, and the whole community to take control of asthma.*

- *Children who participate in Open Airways For Schools do better in school, feel better about themselves, and have fewer and shorter asthma episodes.*

- *The American Lung Association makes it easy for schools and other community organizations to participate in Open Airways For Schools—and at little or no direct cost.*

- *The program consists of six lessons and can be taught by school staff or American Lung Association volunteers during the school day.*

- *The award-winning Open Airways For Schools curriculum and materials are colorful, make learning fun, and are available with English and Spanish handouts and posters.*

- *The American Lung Association web site provides a wealth of related information.*

- *Beyond Open Airways For Schools, the American Lung Association is a resourceful partner with information, education, and community service programs that reduce youth smoking and help ensure a lung-healthy environment for everyone.*

- *To bring Open Airways For Schools to your school or community call 1-800-lung-USA, visit www.lungusa.org or contact your local Lung Association.*

To develop the substance for an effective promotional message, respond to the following:

1. Who is the target audience?

2. How do they best receive information—language and sources?

3. What are the three key benefits of your product?

4. What are the top features and options?

5. What is the call to action?

*Turn to **Section B** of **Worksheet 6,** pages 190–191, and record your answers to the above questions.*

You now have the substance for an overall image and the key messages to be conveyed through your promotion campaign. This informs how all promotional materials and techniques should look and what they should say.

The next step is deciding what materials and techniques you will use—the tools of your promotion campaign.

Promotion Materials and Techniques

Promotion materials and techniques are the actual tools you use to convey your image and message. Your promotion campaign may be modest, employing one or two tools, or you may use a more complex mix with more than a dozen tools. Regardless of the size of your promotion campaign, always keep in mind the highest impact tool of all: personal contact. Complete guidance on one-to-one promotion and making every member of your organization a "marketing representative" is the subject of *Marketing Workbook Volume II: Mobilize People for Marketing Success*. It may be the information age, but there is no substitute for the respect, openness, and trust that is only built on a personal basis.

It may be the information age, but there is no substitute for the respect, openness, and trust that is only built on a personal basis.

Following is a list of promotion tools used by many nonprofits. You can find an annotated version of this list—with comments on each material or technique—in Appendix C.

Promotion tools

Advertising	Letters to the editor	Publishing articles and reports
Annual reports	Marketing partnerships	Signage
Atmosphere and attitude	Networking	Special events
Billboards and transit ads	News conferences	Specialty advertising
Brochures	News releases	Talk shows
Business cards, letterhead, and other essentials	Newsletters	Telemarketing
Celebrity endorsements	Personal contact	Trade fairs
Direct mail	Posters	Videos
Editorials	Presentations, public speaking, and training	Web site
E-mail and broadcast fax	Public service announcements	Word of mouth
Feature stories		

Following are seven principles to help you choose an effective combination of tools for your campaign effort.

1. Gear the materials and techniques to the audience.

Think about how your target audience lives and works, where they go, what they are most likely to look at, listen to, or read, who they respect and pay attention to. Then think about the tools that fit into that picture. Three examples:

a. You might develop the all-time best newspaper ad, but if you want to reach teenagers, you're better off with a spot on MTV, a poster on the subway, and a hot web site.

b. If you want the attention of employers, a detailed brochure is probably good wrapping for a useful batch of Post-it notes that display a logo, slogan, phone number, and web address.

c. Politicians respond to credible expressions of public opinion. If your audience is the state legislature, editorials in leading newspapers and webzines that showcase your work or back up your point of view are persuasive.

2. Plan how each tool can be used to the maximum effect.

Here's a critical issue that people often miss: think right up front about how you will *use and distribute* every tool, especially printed pieces like flyers, posters, and brochures. Will you mail them? What mailing list will you use? Will you hire a fleet of kids to tape them up throughout the neighborhood? Will you adapt them for the web? How else can you get them where they need to go?

In the example of a newspaper editorial, the effect is wasted if the legislators don't see it. In this case, make copies (with permission when required) and *be sure* to get them where they need to be. You might also enlarge the editorial to poster size and hang it in the lobby, bring it along to conferences, feature it on the home web site, or present it as a gift to others who would enjoy it.

3. Pick the right mix of techniques—within your budget.

Don't put all your eggs in one basket. You may have your publics targeted with extreme precision, but even within a narrow group, people have different learning styles and respond best to different approaches. Think about commercial advertising. When a big campaign is underway, you might have the impression the message is *everywhere*. Nonprofits aren't Microsoft or 3M, but you may be able to back up your brochure with interaction on the web, follow-up phone calls, a few well-placed billboards, notices in the newspaper, personal letters, a personal visit, or a presentation at a conference or public forum.

4. Repeat your message frequently over an extended period of time.

This goes along with picking the right mix of tools. Besides using a number of them, reinforce your image and messages as often as you can as long as you can. There is an advertising formula that goes like this:

$$frequency \ over \ time = reach$$

The formula means that promotion messages must be repeated over and over again in order to *get through*.

5. If it worked, do it again.

During your audit, you listed aspects of promotion that worked for you in the past. Updating your image and messages is important to stay with the times and accurately reflect your change and growth. But when you have gotten good response from a particular combination of tools, keep using your winning formula. When response has peaked and begins to decline, then it is time to consider a new approach.

6. Never abandon the basics.

Some nonprofits have been seduced by glamour or thrown off track by success. They have been smart enough or lucky enough—or both—to get extensive media coverage, a hot pro bono advertising campaign, or have in some other way "struck it rich." It's great to be the talk of the town and it's certainly all for the best, but it can make the routine aspects of your promotion campaign seem tedious and unnecessary. No matter how well things seem to be going, never assume you've got it made. Keep up with the basics.

7. Stay the course.

Occasionally a promotion campaign will flop. If that happens, try to understand what went wrong, then move on. Or you may experience modest success, falling somewhat short of your goals. Keep in mind that most successful marketing efforts represent a long-term investment. If your goals are realistic, the marketing plan sound, and your promotion well conceived, you should be able to earn the response you want over time. Remember, Rome wasn't built in a day.

Given finite resources, you probably can't do everything you would like to do in the way of promotion. Consider choices based on what will best help you reach your marketing goals. It's always best to use as many free and low-cost techniques as possible, but there are also times when significant investment is essential. Nonprofits must strike a delicate balance: too much or too flashy can backfire. Nor is constant conservatism necessarily a virtue. Decisions should be made considering both risks and rewards (however, never risk the farm). The bottom line is the mission. If a hefty promotion budget helps further it, then it's money well spent.

Decide what tools to include in your promotion campaign

Some elements of the campaign may already be in place or fairly easy and inexpensive to undertake. Other ideas may require extensive groundwork and coordination. Here again, marketing communications and Internet specialists are helpful. Advice is available on overall campaign concepts, creative approaches, and "the best ways to go." Then, coordinating and implementing the campaign calls for yet another cast of characters.

Marketing communications and Internet specialists may come from inside or outside the organization. Some nonprofits have dedicated staff, outsource to individuals and agencies, and have active volunteer committees. Others tap individual areas of expertise—the counselor with graphic design skills, the gallery crew member who writes ad copy, the web-wizard intern, and so on. For those with less access to specialists, "do-it-yourself" guidance on copywriting and print design follows in Appendix D.

*Go to **Section C** of **Worksheet 6,** page 192. Choose your promotion tools, and note how they will work together to gain the response you want.*

Implementation

Implementing the campaign includes production of materials and follow-through on using each technique. Responsibility for implementation should be decided and deadlines and budgets set. (See Step 4, pages 90–91, for explanations of assigning responsibility, setting deadlines, and confirming a budget.) Those responsible can then develop individual schedules for meeting deadlines in the plan. Be realistic about how long production really takes and be sure to plan sufficient time for things that need to be coordinated, such as setting up the satellite downlink and engraving plaques for the recognition dinner.

*Now complete **Section D** of **Worksheet 6,** page 193, Implementation.* See Appendix D for tips on implementing your promotion plan.

It Takes Money to Make Money—and Further the Mission

The marketing team for a technology career training program for people with disabilities is aiming to fill a class with twelve enrollees. Each eligible participant carries $12,000 in tuition through a federally funded program. While class capacity is eighteen, the program breaks even at twelve and, after three years of experience, enrolling twelve people with the right eligibility and aptitudes is considered success.

Still, the team isn't satisfied. Nearly 15 percent of the adult population could be eligible, but the promotion budget only reaches a sliver. A two-pronged idea comes up: blanket targeted neighborhoods door-to-door with flyers and get way more interactive on the web. Only problem: $25,000 to make it happen. The team makes a business case: if we spend $25,000 and get two additional enrollees, we're almost at break-even. If we get three, then we're $11,000 to the good.

The team makes its case to management. The level of risk is acceptable and the idea is approved. The campaign goes well and class enrollment goes up—to sixteen! The initiative pays off two ways: increased net tuition income and, most important, four more people with disabilities who might never have been reached are now on the road to new careers.

WORKSHEET 6   Develop a Promotion Campaign

SECTION A—Image

An effective image makes the impression you want.

1. Brainstorm a list of colorful and descriptive words or phrases, metaphors,
   or comparisons that reflect your desired image.

   Multicultural

   Familiar and friendly

   Color: red

   Effective

   Medically sound

   TV shows: Sesame Street, The Simpsons

   Makes learning fun

   Authoritative and trustworthy

2. Circle the above items that do the best job of reflecting your desired image.

SECTION B—Message

An effective message prompts your target audience to take a specific action and promises
a valuable benefit if they do.

1. Who is the target audience?

   School nurses and other decision-makers

   Community organization decision-makers

   Volunteers:
   - **Community organizations**
   - **Individual medical professionals**
   - **Nursing, respiratory therapy, pharmacy, and
     other medical schools and associations**

   Funders/sponsors:
   - **Pharmaceutical companies**
   - **Foundations**
   - **Health care organizations**
   - **Corporations**
   - **Small businesses**
   - **Individual donors**

SECTION B—Message (continued)

2. How do they best receive information—language and sources?

All Open Airways For Schools target audiences best receive the type of promotion messages we need to send through in-person meetings, whether one-to-one or at professional association events. The "personal touch"—from peer professionals whenever possible—is essential. Parents of children with asthma are important sources for school decision-makers. Simple written materials are helpful, as well as proposals in formats best suited to each individual audience. Language is uniformly straightforward, professional, and must demonstrate knowledge of communicating well with kids. Some promotion materials should be available in Spanish. The program materials already are.

3. What are the three key benefits of your product that target audiences value most?

1. Increased school performance.
2. Kids' lives change when they manage their asthma better.
3. Good community relations and a chance to make a difference.

4. What are the top features and options?

Easy to use, English or Spanish, short time frame—six sessions, little training needed, proven effective, kids like it and participate eagerly.

5. What is the call to action?

"Do something today to help a child with asthma breathe easier tomorrow."

- **Improve school performance—bring Open Airways For Schools to 4th–6th graders with asthma**

- **Connect with kids—change the life of children with asthma—volunteer to be an Open Airways For Schools teacher**

- **Change the life of a child with asthma—support the Open Airways For Schools program**

(continued)

Section C—Materials and Techniques

The principles for an effective combination are:

(1) Gear tools to the audience.
(2) Plan how each tool can be used to maximum effect.
(3) Pick the right mix—within budget.
(4) Frequency over time equals reach.
(5) If it worked, do it again.
(6) Don't abandon the basics.
(7) Stay the course.

Make the choices you believe will be most effective, keeping in mind budget constraints and how much effort you can realistically put into development and follow-through.

1. Check the promotion tools you will use in your campaign.

- ☑ Advertising
- ☑ Annual reports
- ☐ Atmosphere and attitude
- ☐ Billboards/transit ads
- ☑ Brochures
- ☑ Business cards, letterhead, and other essentials
- ☐ Celebrity endorsements
- ☑ Direct mail
- ☐ Editorials
- ☐ E-mail and fax
- ☑ Feature stories
- ☐ Letters to the editor
- ☑ Marketing partnerships
- ☑ Networking
- ☐ News conference
- ☐ News releases

- ☑ Newsletters
- ☑ Personal contact
- ☐ Posters
- ☑ Presentations, public speaking, and training
- ☐ Public service announcements
- ☑ Publishing articles and reports
- ☐ Signage
- ☐ Special events
- ☐ Specialty advertising
- ☐ Talk shows
- ☑ Telemarketing
- ☐ Trade fairs
- ☐ Videos
- ☑ Web site
- ☑ Word of mouth

2. How will these materials and techniques work together to gain the response you want?

Presentations at professional meetings and conferences will introduce target audiences to Open Airways For Schools. One-to-one contact and follow-up is the centerpiece of the promotion campaign—it is a true relationship-building and "sales" effort. Print materials and a modest public relations plan will support solicitations.

A sample of the actual Open Airways For Schools brochure is shown on pages 118–119.

Worksheet 6—Develop a Promotion Campaign

Section D—Implementation

Notes:

1. All promotion materials for the program are to be developed or obtained in year one.
2. Minimal new materials are projected for following years.
3. Budget column below shows direct costs.
4. All promotion steps require staff time and are fully accounted for in job descriptions and personnel budgets.

Step	Responsibility	Deadline	Budget
1. Purchase 1,000 brochures from National Office.	Director of communications & development (DCD)	3/1	$250
2. Get flyer on disk from National Office, customize content, and produce flyers as needed.	DCD	4/1	In-house photocopying
3. Develop complete information packets for funders, volunteers, and media. Funder packet to include OAS Kit	DCD & program director (PD)	4/1 Funders 5/1 Volunteers 5/1 Media	General office supplies for basic packets. $1,000 (20 kits @ $50/ea.)
4. Develop model funding proposal.	DCD & PD	4/1	None
5. Develop school, funder, and volunteer recruitment presentation outlines.	DCD, PD, program staff	4/1 Schools 5/1 Others	None
6. Begin contacting prospective schools to set up meetings and presentations.	PD & program staff with executive director & board members based on personal contacts	4/1 and ongoing	None
7. Begin contacting prospective funders. As appropriate, send letters of interest and proposals or set up meetings and visits to OAS classes.	DCD, PD, executive director & board members based on personal contacts	5/1 and ongoing	Minimal postage

(continued)

Section D—Implementation (continued)

Step	Responsibility	Deadline	Budget
8. Finalize volunteer recruitment media lists (print and web).	DCD	5/15	None
9. Begin contacting organizations with prospective volunteers to - Obtain mailing lists (some will be complimentary, others may be paid) - Schedule presentations at meetings and conferences - Determine if feature stories or public service ads can be placed in newsletters, intranets, or web sites	PD, program staff, & board members who may belong to targeted organizations	5/15 and ongoing	$250 (estimate)
10. Implement website enhancements	DCD, web master	6/1 - 9/1	$500
11. Develop volunteer recruitment: - Print ad slick - Electronic ad formats - Direct mail cover letter	DCD, web master	6/1	$150
12. Distribute volunteer recruitment media kits and ad slicks as appropriate.	DCD, program staff	6/1 and ongoing	Minimal postage
13. Select and obtain available volunteer recruitment mailing lists and send first wave of direct mail: cover letter and program brochure.	PD, admin. assistant	7/1, 10/1, 2/1 with ongoing assessment of cost-effectiveness	Up to $500 postage and supplies

Section D—Implementation (continued)

Step	Responsibility	Deadline	Budget
14. Phone follow-up with all responsive prospects.	All	Ongoing	None
15. Make in-person presentations with schools, funders, and organizations with prospective volunteers.	All	As scheduled, ongoing	None
16. Pursue feature coverage in mainstream media to coincide with school opening and program graduations	DCD	8/1 and ongoing	None
17. Place program information and feature coverage as possible in all available school media once school signs on.	PD and program staff	Ongoing	None
18. Feature OAS in ALA newsletter, annual report, at special events, and as other related opportunities arise.	DCD, all	Ongoing	None
Contingencies			$350

The following is a black-and-white reproduction of the Open Airways For Schools four-color brochure.

Front panel: *Back panel:*   *First inside panel:*

Inside:

Open Airways For Schools is fun, easy, and most important, *effective!*

ASTHMA is the leading chronic illness in children. More than a million children between 8 and 11 years old suffer from this debilitating disease. Asthma is responsible for missed school days, numerous visits to the doctor or the emergency room, and enormous anxiety for children, parents and educators who struggle with its impact on a child's daily life.

There is no cure for asthma and, for reasons that are not clearly understood, it is on the rise. The good news is that asthma can be controlled and children themselves can do a great deal to manage their condition. But first they must know what steps to take when asthma symptoms develop, how to use medications correctly, and when to seek help from adults.

The American Lung Association's Open Airways For Schools is designed to empower 8-11-year old children and their parents to take control of asthma. This entertaining, interactive program was developed and evaluated by Columbia University's College of Physicians and Surgeons. Open Airways For Schools has a documented track record of success and can be taught by professionals or volunteers. Children who participate in it manage their asthma better, get higher grades and build self-esteem.

Story of George Part 2

It's the beginning of the second half of the basketball game during gym. The physical education (P.E.) teacher talks to George.

Step 5: Do your deep cough

Tensing and Relaxing Exercise

Instead of worrying, what can you do?

" *My daughter told me she was no longer afraid of dying from an asthma attack because now she knows what to do.* "

—Mother of child with asthma

A Open Airways For Schools Instructor's Guide

A school-based asthma health education program for children with asthma

AMERICAN LUNG ASSOCIATION

OPEN AIRWAYS FOR SCHOOLS is now being used in thousands of schools around the country, thanks to the collaborative efforts of school boards, principals, teachers, school nurses, parents, sponsors, and volunteers from a wide range of communities. The ultimate goal is **to reach every child with asthma**, through the nationwide American Lung Association network and with help from countless community partners.

The program consists of six lessons, which are taught during the school day. Each lesson is 40 minutes long and is designed to be easy for trained volunteers or school staff to present. A detailed curriculum, an instructor's guide, plus posters and handouts, make teaching and learning fun for everyone involved.

While asthma strikes children of all backgrounds, minority groups are disproportionately affected. OPEN AIRWAYS FOR SCHOOLS has a distinctive multicultural appeal and is now available with both English and Spanish language text on the handouts and posters.

All over America, communities are mobilizing to help children with asthma take control and succeed. To join in this effort, contact your local American Lung Association or call 1-800-LUNG-USA.

Do something today to help a child with asthma breathe easier tomorrow.

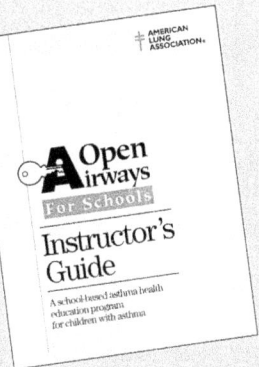

"*Now there's a way for children to deal with the fear that they have when an asthma episode begins, and they don't know whether they can control it.*"

—School Principal

© 1997 American Lung Association

Evaluate Your Marketing Effort

I N MARKETING, like so many things, experience is the best teacher. Regularly track your marketing efforts to evaluate progress and results and make adjustments along the way. Learn from failure, but don't belabor it. Learn from success so you know how to repeat it. Learning, like any achievement, should be celebrated! Then, apply all your new knowledge to the next time out.

Here are seven questions to evaluate a marketing effort:

1. Did you meet your goals?
2. Did you follow your plan—or amend it?
3. What went well?
4. What didn't go so well?
5. What would you do differently next time around?
6. What would you repeat?
7. What are you learning?

Your evaluation process can suit your own needs and style. A roundtable discussion is sufficient for some groups, while others prefer detailed written reports. To be ready to conduct a good evaluation, think ahead and collect information throughout your marketing effort. You may document:

- The final numbers that tell you whether or not you reached your marketing goals
- What went well and what didn't
- How you amended the plan
- How much you spent, including staff time and overhead
- Response to the promotion campaign
- Promotion tools that seemed particularly effective
- Various aspects of visitor activity on your web site

The data you collect should help you determine what worked, what didn't, and where you might need to improve. If evaluation leaves you with more questions than answers, return to the marketing audit and conduct necessary research before revamping your plan.

Open Airways For Schools Succeeds—But Not Quite as Planned

Quite according to plan, the Open Airways For Schools marketing team reconvenes annually to revisit the plan and update it. There is continuous progress, many occasions for celebration, and by adjusting strategy as they learn, ultimate success in meeting ambitious goals. After two years, Jennifer reflects, "There is such a sense of confidence now about what we can do. We learned to think big and proved to ourselves we could do what we set our mind to!"

Here are the results of the two-year assessment of Open Airways For Schools.

1. Did you meet your goals?

Participation	1998	1999	2000
A. Schools goal	25 new/total 30 (maintain 5)	50 new/total 80 (maintain 30)	70 new/total 150 (maintain 80)
Actual:	*15 new/total 20 (maintained 5)*	*20 new/total 40 (maintained 20)*	*Revised goal: 85 new/total 125 (maintain 40)*
B. Children goal	300	800	1,500 Three-year total: 2,600
Actual:	*200*	*400*	*Revised goals: 1,250 Three-year total: 1,850*
C. Parents goal	300	800	1,500
Actual:	*200*	*400*	*Revised goal: 1,250*
D. Volunteers goal	30 new/total 35 (retain 5)	55 new/total 85 (retain 30)	65 new/total 140 (retain 75)
Actual:	*20 new/total 23 (retained 3)*	*55 new/total 75 (retained 20)*	*Revised goal: 48 new/total 115 (retain 67)*
E. Funding goal	$50,000	$120,000	$120,000
Actual:	*$100,000*	*$200,000*	*Three-year goal: $290,000*

Comments:

We had very mixed experiences in terms of meeting our goals. Funding was clearly our biggest success. We got an early challenge grant for $150,000, which put us on the map and on the way. We were able to raise matching funds right on schedule so we finished year two *ahead* of goal. On the other hand, we're behind in signing on new schools. We discovered it took much more effort to maintain a school than we projected. We decided to concentrate on keeping the customers we had and delivering quality for kids before moving on. Our revised sales plan for new schools in year three is very aggressive, but we've got the staff and the understanding to do it. We'll be a little short of goal overall, but we've gone over things with our funders and they have endorsed our approach. Volunteer recruitment has gone well—we're right on target.

2. Did you follow your plan—or amend it?

We followed it in some ways, but not in others. We didn't come to terms early enough with our shift from signing on new schools to the demanding work of maintaining existing ones. So the plan changed and now we will have to be *very* sales oriented to catch up. At the two-year point, we held an intensive all-day planning session to map out year three. The plan is now officially amended.

3. What went well?

Grantseeking! Also, building new relationships with schools and volunteers, which resulted in new schools coming to us and new partnerships with institutions that have a pool of volunteers. The general community and the public health sector see the American Lung Association as a leader in pediatric asthma education. This has resulted in more support for our organization's efforts, including unexpected funding from tobacco tax dollars for the program. We got good support from the national organization. The four-color brochure is great. We wouldn't have been able to afford it on our own.

4. What didn't go so well?

We haven't developed faculty or parent education curricula as we intended. We did a few information sessions but haven't created the same kind of high-quality experience that Open Airways For Schools offers to kids. The whole approach needs rethinking. Also, we fell a bit behind in selling the program to schools. We underestimated our own learning curve and how much work it takes to maintain the various relationships at one school to keep the program going.

5. What would you do differently next time around?

We would find ways to be more efficient earlier. At the same time we would add more staff earlier in the effort. We would add to the budget incentives for volunteers instead of trying to get in-kind donations—that approach was just more trouble than it was worth. We'd stop sooner to assess what *maintenance* really means, so we wouldn't lose momentum in other areas. As soon as we succeeded with funding, we would invest in building up staff and expanding efforts.

6. What would you repeat?

Our approach to selling this product. We truly included our customers in the process of tailoring the program to their setting and made sure they felt essential to its success. We understood early on how important the relationships were and we would repeat this emphasis. The funding strategy worked well too. Going in with a three-year plan attracted a funder willing to think big. Our approach of recruiting volunteers through professional networks is a success. There is so much enthusiasm now for Open Airways For Schools that we're discussing inviting customers to form a program growth advisory committee.

7. What are you learning?

How important the marketing audit is—and going back and covering in-depth details. We didn't know our product at the beginning like we do now. Really knowing what your product is, how much it costs, and what it takes to produce it saves you time and helps you reach your goals. We also are learning how important it is to stop, assess progress, and regroup. The world out there is so dynamic—plans have to be alive. We also see the value of thinking ahead and are working hard right now to line up funding for years four, five, and beyond. We are just learning that our current school customers, including administration, kids, and parents, can be real allies in pursuing funding.

Adjustments at the two-year point: We're going to completely make up ground in the schools/kids/faculty/parents goal area, including a look at how we might use our web site to deliver information to parents and faculty. Maintenance is all smoothed out, we've got the interest out there, and we have a strong staff that is absolutely committed to "selling the program." We're working out the action plan details, but it's there—we can do it. We'll be at 125 schools by the end of 2000.

Also this year, we're going to bring the products for parents and faculty to the level they need to be. It's Open Airways For *Schools* and that means the whole school community. The best thing continues to be results with kids. The number may be temporarily behind, but local evaluations are underscoring what this program has done from the beginning: it improves kids' lives—and with a little help from us, that markets itself.

Afterword

A S YOUR marketing effort takes root, it will build on itself. What initially seemed difficult and overwhelming will later take half the time and produce even better results. You will need to be flexible. Through marketing you are opening your doors in a new way and perhaps wider than before. You may be more forthright about what you have to offer, clearer about the reputation and results you want, and respond more individually to deliver value to others. Your organization and your impact may grow—rapidly.

Marketing is a time-tested discipline. Those who practice it well flourish with it. Marketing can help your organization be a leader making a real difference in your community and beyond. It can help you seize opportunity and run with it. Frances Hesselbein, former CEO of the Girl Scouts of the USA and founding president of the Peter F. Drucker Foundation for Nonprofit Management, paints this picture for nonprofits:

> *In this period of unprecedented worldwide societal transformation, remarkable opportunities exist for those who would lead their enterprises and this country into a new kind of community. These leaders will dare to see life and community whole. They will strive to address the needs of the spirit, the mind, and the body. They will view their work as an amazing opportunity to express everything within that gives passion and light to living, and will have the courage to lead from the front on issues, principles, vision, and mission that become the star to steer by. They will change lives.*[15]

Nonprofit leadership produces visions that often run ahead of what others believe is possible. A protected planet. An end to hunger. Loving care for all children. Education, art, and faith that ennoble the spirit. As curators of such visions, the nonprofit marketing task is great. Therein lies the challenge: to light a fire to our promises, to loudly sing their beauty and their value, to open our doors to all who might benefit, and to keep pounding the pavement every day.

In the words of Henry David Thoreau: "If you have built castles in the air, your work need not be lost; that is where they should be. Now put foundations under them."

---

[15] Peter F. Drucker, *The Drucker Foundation Self-Assessment Tool Participant Workbook* (San Francisco: Jossey-Bass, 1999) page v.

Idea-Generating Techniques

Brainstorming

Brainstorming is a way to quickly generate a large number of ideas and involves several ground rules. If working with a group, you will need a leader. That person states specifically what you will be brainstorming about and writes the topic or question at the top of a piece of flip chart paper or on a chalkboard. The leader then encourages the group to generate as many responses as possible. For example, if you are working on your organization's image, you might want to brainstorm by asking, what are colorful and descriptive words, phrases, metaphors, or comparisons that reflect our desired image?

Here are brainstorming ground rules:

- Keep the ideas coming; don't stop to analyze or discuss.
- Every idea is a good idea; don't criticize or edit.
- Let go and be creative; anything's OK to say, no matter how off the wall.

Sometimes brainstorming goes better when you break a big question into smaller parts and brainstorm each part separately. You might do a series of word associations ("what's the first word or phrase that comes to mind when I say..."). Or, as in the example above, you might first respond with words, then phrases, then metaphors, then comparisons such as, "When you think of our image, what color comes to mind? What animal? What TV show? What car?"

When brainstorming is finished, have a short discussion to highlight the "best stuff" that comes out of the exercise.

Visualization

In visualization, people imagine a scene and add in their own dialogue. Here are two possible uses:

For goal-setting, imagine you are attending a celebration for your organization in the future, perhaps two, three, or ten years from now. The reason for the event is to recognize the wonderful success you have achieved as a result of your marketing efforts. The mayor of your city gets up to give a rousing laudatory speech. What is said? What accomplishments are noted?

To use this technique to help get at your positioning statement, imagine you are talking with a person you don't know well. Perhaps it's someone you meet at a party or a new neighbor. The subject is your work and the other person says, "Oh yes, I've heard of your organization. Now what exactly is it that you do?" You respond, "Oh, we're the people who _____ ."

Try not to edit your thoughts. Write down the first things that come to mind in the visualization. You can edit them later.

Timed Writing or Drawing

Timed writing or drawing helps you tap into "stream-of-consciousness." At the top of a blank piece of paper write the topic about which you want to generate ideas. Check the time, give yourself two minutes, and no matter what the first things are that go on the paper, just start and don't stop until two minutes are up. Some people will want to write, others draw pictures or diagrams, and some may do both.

You will wind up with lots of material—some slightly embarrassing, some pretty good. If you're working alone, polish up the good stuff and shred the rest. If it's a group activity, ask a few volunteers to interpret their work, discuss where you're heading, and pass all the raw material to a specified writer for work on a final edited piece.

Market Research

QUESTIONS for market research may come up at any point in the marketing planning process. The primary purpose for conducting research is *to get answers that help you make sound marketing decisions.* Good data helps you avoid marketing mistakes and protects you from the most dangerous pitfall: operating on untested assumptions.

A secondary purpose for market research may be relationship-building. When you go directly to current or potential partners or customers and ask for their input, it suggests you are open, responsive, and interested in what people have to say—a strong step for any organization committed to furthering exchange relationships.

Market research does not always mean going directly to target audiences with your questions. It may require searching out facts, figures, or reports that already exist, collecting examples and best practice information, and even test marketing: implementing a plan and learning from what happens.

Some people fear that directly asking customers what they value will create unrealistic expectations or somehow put customers "too much in charge." The fear is partially grounded: customers should not be asked if they would value something you could never deliver. More often, customers clarify our understanding of what is necessary and stimulate a fresh vision of what is possible. What happens then is up to you.

Steve Jobs, who cofounded Apple Computer and presided over its "think different" rebirth campaign, says this on market research:

> *I think really great products come from melding two points of view—the technology point of view and the customer point of view. You need both. You can't just ask customers what they want and then try to give that to them. By the time you get it built, they'll want something new.... And customers can't anticipate what the technology can do. They won't ask for things that they think are impossible.* [16]

---

[16] Steve Jobs, "Entrepreneur of the Decade, an Interview with Steve Jobs," in *Inc.* (April, 1989) page 114.

The most important thing at the outset of market research is to be clear on what questions you want answered. Then, to really benefit from the results, bring your own insights and expertise and be ready to learn with an open mind.

Here are a number of subjects frequently addressed by market research:

- **Market demographics**
  How many people are out there within our target audiences? How do these audiences break down in terms of age, gender, race, economic status, sexual orientation, or other characteristics? How is the market changing?

- **Market capacity**
  How much is out there for us? Is opportunity huge or fairly limited? At what levels might individuals or groups respond?

- **Competition**
  Who else is out there asking for exchanges similar to ours? What do they offer? How are they doing? How do we compare? Could these competitors become partners?

- **Exemplary models**
  What is being done that we might learn from? What organizations and products are really setting standards for tomorrow, on the Internet and in other channels?

- **Customer reality**
  What are our customers' lives really like? What do they value? What are their *needs* (physical and psychological well-being)? What are their *wants* (immediate interests; where, when, and how service is provided)? What are their *aspirations* (desired long-term results)? What motivates people? What really excites them? What turns them off?

- **Production**
  What are the best organizational models for marketing planning and implementation? Who can we learn from to develop the most efficient and effective processes? How have others assured their ability to meet demand?

- **Customer service**
  What are people's bottom line expectations of us? What must we do to delight every customer every time?

- **Effective promotion**
  What works that we can study and learn from? How do members of our target audiences best receive information? What combination of tools will be affordable and effective?

- **Customer satisfaction**
  What pleases and displeases our customers? How might we improve?

Here are a number of options for conducting market research:

Note: before you embark on any level of market research, make sure you think through how the information you obtain will be compiled, analyzed, and summarized to make it useful.

1. **Ask around.**

   It is surely not the most scientific method, but sometimes a few well-placed phone calls, web site visits, or interviews give you just what you need. You may choose to take what you learn at face value or test the feedback with a wider audience.

2. **Look close to home.**

   If your questions have to do with customer reality, customer service, or customer satisfaction, you can learn from the people you already know. Here are suggestions:

   - Regularly invite your customers to recommend how you might improve.

   - Follow up with people who show initial interest in your product but don't sign on.

   - Conduct exit interviews with people who quit programs midway, don't renew season tickets, or in other ways sever their relationship with you.

   - Look for patterns in why people who apply aren't accepted to your programs.

   - Ask frontline staff, especially those who answer phones and e-mail, for their observations.

3. **Check with known data collectors.**

   There are plenty of organizations and web sites that collect and report on all kinds of data. If you have market research questions on nearly any subject, you can find out a lot by contacting

   - The United Way and other nonprofit umbrella groups

   - The Census Bureau and many other government agencies

   - Research organizations

   - Industry organizations (Independent Sector, American Association of Museums, Child Welfare League of America, Energize Inc. [on volunteerism], National Society of Fundraising Executives, and so forth)

   - Public libraries

   - Colleges and universities

   - Marketing agencies and associations, including list brokers

   - Media organizations

4. Conduct surveys.

Written, telephone, Internet-based, and in-person surveys can tell you a tremendous amount about market capacity, customer reality, customer service, effective promotion, customer satisfaction, and more. For a survey to produce reliable information, however, it must be well designed. *Do-It-Yourself Marketing Research*[17] is an accessible and easy-to-follow book for doing just what it says. If you would rather *not* do it yourself, input and assistance is often available from

- Current board members, volunteers, or people they know
- Nonprofit technical assistance organizations and consultants
- Marketing agencies
- Graduate interns
- Corporate marketing departments
- Government agencies

Sometimes, a little outside advice is all that's needed. In other cases, hiring a professional team is critical.

5. Hold focus groups.

Focus group research provides valuable qualitative information on a range of potential topics. It works like this: A representative sample of a target audience (ten to twelve people is an ideal group size) is brought together to participate in a discussion usually no longer than one hour. The session produces responses to a predetermined question path and is facilitated by an outsider or member of the organization who can elicit open discussion. The format is carefully structured to gain straightforward impressions, reactions, and opinions. Judy Sharken-Simon's book *The Fieldstone Alliance Nonprofit Guide to Conducting Successful Focus Groups*[18] is an excellent resource on focus group research.

The major attraction of focus group research is that it puts you *directly* in touch with target audiences in a way that allows you to hear subtleties in people's language and how their thoughts develop in discussion with others. You can learn

- What people value and why
- What people dislike
- Positive ideas for change
- What image and messages strike a positive chord
- What people would do about marketing your organization or product if they were you
- How to speak in the language of your audience (which can sometimes provide exact wording for promotion messages)

---

[17] George Breen and A. B. Blankenship, *Do-It-Yourself Marketing Research* (New York: McGraw-Hill, Inc., 1982).

[18] Judith Sharken-Simon, *The Fieldstone Alliance Nonprofit Guide to Conducting Successful Focus Groups* (St. Paul: Fieldstone Alliance, 1999).

The major drawback to focus group research is the relatively small sample size. While focus group research may lack the statistical reliability of larger samples, it does tell you a great deal about what participants think. To confirm what you learn, you may wish to increase the scope of focus group research or test preliminary findings through other, more quantitative means.

Focus groups do not need to be time-consuming or costly. Facilitation is often quite easily obtained free of charge or can be handled with minimal training of qualified staff. Even when you hire professionals, a modest focus group project is relatively affordable.

6. Test market.

Sometimes you just do it. No matter how thorough or sound your market research, nothing tells you as much as how people actually respond. When you believe your marketing plan is as shipshape as it can be, you may float it through a small-scale pilot, enlist a specially selected "test audience," or even launch it exactly as planned with specific research objectives and opportunities for learning and adjustment built in. The greater the scope or risk associated with a marketing plan, the more reason for focused test marketing—and for solid market research overall.

Again, *the most important things to know about market research are what information you are after and how you will use it.* If you need help deciding what research techniques will be most effective in getting that information—and within your budget and timelines—ask for advice from many of the same resources listed above.

Market research as relationship-builder

Whenever you go out to the community and ask questions—especially if you are asking current or potential partners or customers directly—it is an opportunity to engage people in a positive way and build relationships. Most folks enjoy the opportunity to express their opinions and will think well of you for asking. It may also add to their interest or enthusiasm for your organization or product.

Think through how your research efforts can also be relationship-builders. Here are a few tips and considerations:

1. Be well prepared, gracious, and professional. Don't be afraid to offer appropriate perks for participating: pizza dinner, entry for a prize drawing, even a modest stipend or honorarium.

2. Follow up immediately on any individual interests, questions, or concerns and make your ultimate research findings available to all participants.

3. Provide opportunities, when appropriate, for research participants to get more involved with your organization through consumer advisory groups or other volunteer opportunities.

4. If you're conducting research on a brand new offering, be sure to reach out to research participants and invite their participation when the product is available.

5. Thank and acknowledge research participants directly and, when warranted, report on your research effort and findings through your web site, newsletters, annual report, presentations to the board, volunteers, and staff, or in other useful ways.

Annotated List of Promotional Techniques

Advertising

Great if you can afford it, but generally considered ineffective in small doses. Advertising can work well for special or seasonal events. Some print media make free space available; most electronic media offer public service time. If you *purchase* space or time (always best when possible), ask for nonprofit discounts. Classified ads and web banners are a low-cost advertising option. Think about inserting flyers in community newspapers when you want to reach broad audiences.

Annual reports

Often considered a must. Be sure to think of this as both a positioning and promotion tool and apply a marketing approach. How many different ways can you use it? Can it take the place of an overall brochure, especially if your organization changes a lot year by year? Pay close attention to image, address where you are going, not just where you have been, consider innovative approaches, think through distribution.

Atmosphere and attitude

The first impression you make should reflect your overall commitment to quality and service. Think about how your phone is routinely answered. Do people get the feeling you are glad they called? Do they feel welcomed to your web site? How are people greeted when they physically come into your organization? The atmosphere should be pleasant and comfortable, the staff courteous and helpful. Here's a test: if you have a sign at the door, does it say "Welcome!" or "Visitors must sign in"?

Billboards and transit ads

Public service programs in many areas make billboards and transit ads very affordable. Check with individual companies for rates and availability. Get a good design and use few words. An excellent way to reach certain target audiences.

Brochures

Your organizational business card. Not every program needs one—flyers, fact sheets, and other options will do. Think through shelf life and distribution, pay close attention to image and message, *enlist professional level talent for copywriting and design,* and remember, most of us look at the pictures and glance through the headlines.

Business cards, letterhead, and other essentials

Generally found in the office supplies budget and should always be thought of from a marketing point of view. Beyond bare necessities, do they convey your image? The right message? Be thoughtful about this category, but don't give it more than its due. Buy in quantity.

Celebrity endorsements

Fun, worthwhile, and a lot of work. (One nonprofit exec lamented, "Well, I wanted a star!") Unless they're also big donors and attract their friends, don't expect much. This is an attention-getter, but seldom in and of itself "makes the sale."

Direct mail

Varies widely in effectiveness both in print and on the web. If you are considering using this extensively, take a seminar to learn the details. It is really a science. Two tips: (1) Direct mail works best once someone already knows who you are and has expressed some interest in you. (2) Good use of lists is essential—testing if you rent or buy them, keeping them updated if you maintain your own. Direct mail is often used as an "acquisition technique" with an investment/return mindset. Once you start a relationship, odds are good it may prove worthwhile long term.

Editorials

Editors are remarkably accessible and will consider well thought out, well documented points of view. Make a phone call or send an e-mail first and be prepared to forward information right away if you get a positive response. Offers high visibility, is an excellent positioning tool for your organization, and is a real contribution to public debate on important issues.

E-mail and fax

Ideal for advance notice and follow-up reminders. In some cases, these are the preferred way of receiving news and a range of marketing messages. A low-cost medium, e-mail often surpasses the phone as the next best thing to being there—only beware of too much of a good thing.

Feature stories

Reporters are looking for news. If you have something timely, unique, interesting, or new, give it a try. They like a fresh angle, aren't afraid to say no, and may put you off repeatedly for months and then suddenly be on deadline and want to talk to you at one o'clock in the morning. Don't say *anything* you wouldn't want to hear on the news or read in print tomorrow morning. Think through how to gain the maximum effect of feature coverage and be prepared for high-volume, short-lived response.

Letters to the editor

When timely, well thought out, short, and well written, they are very often published. Don't be shy. If you have a strong opinion, a positive solution, or your position is being attacked, undermined, or misrepresented by others, get in there and write! It's a good positioning tool. Your friends and allies will appreciate you for doing this. Like feature coverage, think through how to gain maximum effect.

Marketing partnerships

An important and growing phenomenon, both inside the nonprofit sector and crossing boundaries with business and government. Whether driven by the sheer scope of your issues, cost efficiencies, or following consumer trends favoring good corporate citizenship, partnerships can greatly enhance the depth and reach of a marketing plan. To start one, think who shares the same target audiences you do, whose reputation you'd be proud to share, what you and your partner might offer each other, and how you will propose the idea. If this is new territory, read up on it or get counsel from someone who's been there. Time-consuming and dicey though they can be, partnerships at every level of marketing can make sense and make an impact.

Networking

The old saying is true: It's not what you know, but who you know, that matters. Marketing is all about relationships. If you're not an extrovert, pretend. Who you know can mean everything in terms of *access*. Go to conferences, meetings, and events. Ask colleagues, board members, volunteers, distant relatives, and good friends to introduce you, host gatherings, and otherwise connect you with who you need to know.

News conferences

Use news conferences only for something very big, very controversial, or very out of the ordinary. If there is anything you can do to make it visually interesting it will help extend coverage. Prepare your materials and messages carefully. Hope it's a slow news day.

News releases

Can announce anything at all, and will often be run if they get to the right person at the right time. Learn everyone's deadlines and who to address releases to. Check any basic public or media relations textbook for the appropriate professional format. It's very good to announce classes, workshops, conferences, special events, and to get in the news if you've won awards, hired new management staff, or otherwise have something simple and newsworthy to convey. Don't be above gimmicks. The extra-special news release hanging from a helium balloon gets noticed. Costs are paper, envelopes, stamps, and people's time.

Newsletters

Virtual or paper? Maybe both. Newsletters let people know you are alive and well and, when they deliver value in themselves, can produce loyal readers and good response. Keep them regular. Unless eagerly awaiting content, most people only scan newsletters, so use lots of pictures, headlines, sub-headlines, boxes, pull-out quotes, and white space.

Personal contact

Arguably the best promotion technique of all, very labor intensive, and most applicable when the personal touch is essential. There is a sales truism: "People buy from people." Mobilizing everyone associated with your organization as "marketing representatives" is the single most available and powerful means of promotion. For all the details, see *Marketing Workbook for Nonprofit Organizations Volume II: Mobilize People for Marketing Success*.

Posters

Location is critical. Posters are a wonderful way to reflect image. Like billboards and transit ads, they are a great way to mix media. A secondary benefit to attractive posters is their staying power. When suitable for framing, they hang around for years.

Presentations, public speaking, and training

Don't just attend conferences, give training sessions! Or get out and speak to your local civic clubs, religious auxiliaries, or any other likely forum. If you need it, get coaching or training in order to be a solid presenter. (Nearly every pro has had a coach.) Speaking and training are good positioning tools and often a free or low-cost way to promote your cause. Some promotion plans call for development of a scripted presentation with a complete audiovisual package. If this is something you really need, don't scrimp! At minimum, have some good take-home materials to remind people who you are and what you had to say.

Publishing articles and reports

When writing for someone else's audience, be sure you know the reader and gear the article accordingly. If you're looking at a big-time publication or web site, make a study of how to get your work accepted. Self-published reports should have crisp executive summaries and be readable. Showcased or self-published, be clear on your key messages and what you want people to think, feel, and do as a result of seeing them. These are excellent positioning tools and sometimes a real opportunity to influence both professional practice and public thought. Plus, they are something to send home to mom.

Signage

Like business cards, letterhead, and other essentials, signage should always be considered from the marketing point of view. Signs convey both image and message. They say, "Here we are!" Aside from those for whom a subtly or completely unmarked location is a sad but true necessity, who doesn't want to see their name in lights? Other decisions: how big, how many, in what exact spots, for how little money?

Special events

Before you do anything else, set draft marketing goals for the event, run it through a mini-marketing audit, and develop a marketing plan. This is a good way to gain or renew personal contacts on a large scale. Special events can be strong image-builders. Beware of special events as quick fundraising schemes—and account for *all* the costs. Sometimes, they're just spectacular! Expect a sense of relief when it's over.

Specialty advertising

What'll they think of next—more fun and low-cost options every season! From Post-its printed with your logo to thank-you notes with jelly beans inside to pricey bald eagle statuettes, there are catalogs and web sites guaranteed to delight. Check your Yellow Pages. Ask about nonprofit discounts. Get a little carried away.

Talk shows

Radio, television, and the web offer many opportunities for everything from offbeat opinions to live public service announcements to serious discussion. Call or e-mail and talk to the producer of the show. Think through your pitch—why this person should have you on their show. If you do get on, write down ahead of time the three things you absolutely want to be sure to convey. Then, no matter what you are asked, find a way to say them. If you've never done this, seek a coach and practice first. Yes, it's awful, but practice on tape and review your own performance. Depending on the popularity of the show, you can get significant, although short-lived, response. Talk shows are another great way to mix media, and you can go a long way playing the clips.

Telemarketing

Fancy language for using the phone. Like direct mail, this is a numbers game and something of a science. Few people have anything good to say about telemarketing, but lots of people keep doing it because it works. Look for a seminar to get better educated. Market research calls are more welcome than a sales pitch, people are more receptive if they already know you, and some folks have wonderful experiences just calling to say "Thank you!" for something people already have done.

Public service announcements (PSAs)

Think radio, TV, and the web. Think combining PSAs with a paid schedule of advertisements when possible. Check a basic public relations text for professional formatting and each possible media outlet for specific requirements—they vary amazingly and are critical to follow. For most radio stations use written copy only. Prepare thirty, fifteen, and ten seconds worth of copy. Before you go to the trouble of producing a television PSA, make sure you know its chances of getting on. TV stations like PSAs that look like real commercials, so anything you can do to make the grade will help. Again, lengths from five to sixty seconds may be right. Don't forget community cable as a place to make them and show them. As for the web, spend some time surfing to see what's happening, then craft your approach. The rules can change fast. Regardless of the media, relationship-building and follow-up pay off. As do thank-you notes.

Trade fairs

Few people expect to make deals at trade fairs; the people you get to know best are the other people who exhibit. The purpose is to be visible and make *contact*. Be sure to have a way to get people's names and addresses. It's the follow-up that can produce the best results. Have a goody at your booth and a take-away item with your name on it that people will be likely to keep and use. (See *Specialty Advertising* on the previous page.)

Videos

Good video is a definite plus. Look at a video as part of an overall promotional presentation, never in place of one. It is difficult to get free video production, and costs for good video are steep. Sometimes, a poor video is worse than none. When well thought out and used, a strong video may be worth the investment.

Web site

The reach of the world wide web transcends all other media and, with emerging technologies, the digital divide may soon be a thing of the past. Even the most expensively designed and maintained sites are within the budgetary realm of large nonprofit organizations while Internet lore abounds with stories of people who changed the world from their basement. Basic "web wisdom" has been provided throughout this book, and greater knowledge is as accessible as the web itself.

Word of mouth

Long acknowledged as the best kind of advertising, but how do you get it? Three ways. First, by doing what you do *so well* that people are excited and want to talk about it. Second, by making sure everyone associated with your organization is informed, enthusiastic, and pleased to tell anyone and everyone *they* know about who you are and the great things you do. Third, by specifically asking every current customer to pass the good word along, and, as appropriate, providing them with promotion tools to help them do it.

Tips for Implementing Your Promotion Plan

1. Give someone final say.

There are many decisions throughout the process of developing and producing promotion tools. While group input is often valuable, someone has to be able to sign off on things and officially declare them ready to go.

2. You may be a pro bono candidate.

Some aspects of promotion campaigns are appealing pro bono projects for web and traditional marketing agencies and individual professionals. The attraction is threefold: the chance to do creatively interesting work, to see that work make a difference on important issues, and to gain recognition for excellent campaigns. Pro bono assistance is a great way to get top-notch stuff and stretch your promotion budget. Most free assistance is in the area of creative services, and there are often production costs (typesetting, film and processing, software, printing) attached. Make sure you are aware of the roles, responsibilities, and obligations in a pro bono arrangement, and be clear right up front about any special sensitivities you need honored in a pro bono campaign.

3. If it worked in Philadelphia...

Many nonprofits have gotten wonderful materials and saved considerable amounts of time and money by borrowing from other groups in different parts of the country. Keeping up to date in professional networks can produce opportunities of this kind.

4. Consider hiring professionals.

You may have the talent and expertise on staff to produce terrific promotion tools. But if you don't, the services of marketing communications and Internet specialists make all the difference. This kind of help can be pricey, but many people will reduce their fees for nonprofits. Check references and only work with people you like and trust.

5. Shop with care.

Hire a printer, designer, writer, web designer, or mug supplier carefully. It's standard practice for suppliers to make presentations and be interviewed competitively. Look for how well your specific needs can be met, and ask for bids, as prices can vary widely. If you're not sure where to start, call someone more experienced for advice.

6. Take advantage of your suppliers' expertise.

You may not be up on the latest trends, techniques, or innovative notions, but the suppliers you use will be. Make sure to invite input, ideas, and advice. You can build your own knowledge base and continually add creativity and spark to your promotion tools.

7. Reduce costs by coordinating production.

The more you can think ahead on promotion materials, the greater the possibilities of saving money. There are many economies of scale to be had in design, printing, and purchasing of specialty items. Try to coordinate production of any "families" of materials and look into the advantages of stocking up in advance.

8. Plan backward from deadlines.

When you have a deadline, do your production planning backward from that date. For example, if a brochure on a new program needs to be in people's mailboxes by September 1, allow ten days for bulk mailing, one week for mail processing, two weeks for printing, four weeks for graphic design, two weeks for copywriting, one week for content planning, and one week for contingencies. That means you should be starting by June 3. Yes, it can be done faster, but why take chances?

9. Get training and support.

There are many opportunities to build your skill in all aspects of promotion. Excellent one-day training workshops are offered by national as well as local experts. Aside from formal training, look for a promotion mentor. Such a person may work in an advertising or public relations agency, be with a corporation or another nonprofit, or be retired from the field. There is a lot of acquired wisdom in this area, and it is extremely helpful to have someone to turn to for advice.

10. Enjoy!

Promotion can (and should) be fun! It taps your creativity and yields tangible and exciting rewards. You are sure to encounter frustrations, but when success comes along, take a break and bask in it.

If you are producing promotion tools yourself, here are additional tips for writing and design.

Writing Tips

1. **Find examples** of promotion tools you admire and analyze what makes them work for *you*.

2. **Write in the language of the marketplace.** It's effective, permitted, and encouraged to violate the rules of good grammar when writing promotional copy. Ads do it all the time. You can even start a sentence with the words *but* or *and. Really.*

3. **Use headlines to convey the essentials** of your message and don't forget *the promise of a benefit.*

4. **Keep headlines simple.** That's it.

5. **Vary sentence length and structure** in your writing. There are many elements to good copy. This is an important one. After you write a rough draft, check it for rhythm and variety. A good way to do this is to read aloud to yourself (close the door first) or collar a friendly listener.

6. **Emphasize benefits** in all your copy and only include information on the most important features or options of your product.

7. **Give yourself enough time** so you can finish a draft, put it all aside for a few days, and then give it a fresh look before it's out the door.

8. **Show what you write or design to a number of people** and get their reactions and input.

9. **Don't hesitate to do one final edit** to make the copy as short and to the point as possible. Take out extra words.

Print Design Tips

1. **Keep your eye out for current design trends.** Look at all sorts of magazines and web sites to see what's being done, and get a feel for what you think looks good.

2. **Make sure your design calls attention to what is most important**, is free of clutter, and helps the copy be as readable as possible.

3. **White space is great.** There is no need to fill up all the space with writing or design. Blank space helps focus the eye on what's important. A page full of copy can look too overwhelming and turn off the reader.

4. **Use clip art.** An unprecedented global array of lettering, drawings, and pictures is available via CD-ROM and on the web.

5. **Don't use too much art** (especially clip art). A little goes a long way in this department. Avoid a busy look, and don't stick a picture in a white spot just to fill it up.

6. **Use typefaces carefully—and creatively.** Typeface is an expression of your image. Most folks choose one or two standards for the organization and allow only limited variations. Of course certain images mean breaking all the rules, especially those having to do with type. One rule not to break is size. For people over age forty, twelve-point type is a minimum and up from there is better.

7. **Use accents—with care.** Accents are italics, bolds, boxes, rules, screens, colors, and a range of special (often expensive) treatments. These are used as attention-getters. Used artfully, they do the job. Overused, they lose their punch.

8. **Consider helpful software.** Plentiful and varied for beginner and advanced professionals alike. Think through what you'd like to be able to do, survey what's out there, and get advice from more seasoned friends.

9. **Step back from your piece for an overall look.** When it's in final draft form, step back and pretend you are looking at it for the first time. See how all the elements work together.

10. **Go to workshops.** There are excellent workshops on all aspects of promotion—producing newsletters, direct mail, typography, writing copy, and more. Look into local courses at colleges, universities, and technical schools as well as seminars presented across the country by professional training firms. Training is sometimes pricey, but often worth it.

Resources

Business @ the Speed of Thought, Bill Gates with Collins Hemingway. New York: Warner Books, 1999.

> Love him or hate him, if you want a deeper grasp of the digital nervous system underlying everything 'e', read this one.

The Discipline of Market Leaders, Michael Treacy and Fred Wiersema. Reading, MA: Perseus Books, 1995.

> An insightful "macro" view of marketing. This book takes some mental translation from the for-profit context, but is right-on in terms of defining and explaining what market leadership really demands.

Do-It-Yourself Market Research, George Breen and A. B. Blankenship, 3rd edition. Somerville, NJ: Replica Books, 1998.

> Do try this at home. Advice for the nonprofessional marketing researcher on how to run simple, low-cost research studies. Although geared more to businesses, nonprofits can adapt the same techniques.

The Drucker Foundation Self-Assessment Tool, Peter F. Drucker and Gary J. Stern. New York: Jossey-Bass Publishers, 1999.

> The "Drucker Method" of organizational self-assessment poses the key marketing questions, "Who is our customer?" and "What does the customer value?" as overarching strategic questions for the whole organization. If you want marketing firmly integrated within your strategic plan, consider this powerful and energizing approach.

Handbook for Public Relations Writing: The Essentials of Style and Format, *4th edition,* Thomas H. Bivins. New Canaan, CT: Business Books, 1999.

> Comprehensive, cogent, and full of useful specifics for communications in all media. In short, the title says it all.

The Jossey-Bass Guide to Strategic Communications for Nonprofits, Kathy Bonk, Henry Griggs, and Emily Tynes. San Francisco: Jossey-Bass Publishers, 1999.

This book offers detailed suggestions for communicators at every level of experience. It includes case studies on everything from writing a press release to avoiding a news conference. Most important, this book is *smart* and a helpful guide for any nonprofit wishing to advance its mission through communications.

Kotler on Marketing, Philip Kotler. New York: The Free Press, 1999.

Condensed and more accessible than his many texts, this sophisticated primer lays out the science and art that underpin marketing success. Includes a section titled, "Transformational Marketing—Adapting to the New Age of Electronic Marketing." Professor Kotler was voted the First Leader in Marketing Thought by the American Marketing Association. Kotler is The Man.

Managing the Non-Profit Organization, Peter F. Drucker. New York: HarperBusiness, 1990.

Widely considered the "father of modern management," Drucker strikes deep chords in this book, which includes a great interview with Philip Kotler, arguably a "father of nonprofit marketing." From time to time, it's good to sit at the feet of the masters.

Marketing Social Change: Changing Behavior to Promote Health, Social Development, and the Environment, Alan R. Andreasen, San Francisco, Jossey-Bass Publishers, 1995.

The #1 thought leader on social marketing, Andreasen telescopes market research and marketing planning to the specific and intimate behavior changes that add up to broad-scale social change. Simultaneously academic and accessible, this book illuminates the science and skills behind success.

Ogilvy on Advertising, David Ogilvy. New York: Random House Publishers, Inc., 1987.

The essential advertising text by the acknowledged "creative king of the advertising world." His advertising wisdom is as pertinent today as it was in 1987 and as valid for nonprofits as it is for Procter & Gamble.

The Popcorn Report, Faith Popcorn. New York: HarperBusiness, 1991.

At this point, this reads as something of a look back; however, grasping marketplace trends from the Popcorn point of view remains illuminating. Faith keeps popping up so watch for new insights, but in the meantime, salt to taste, grab a soft drink, and dig in.

Selling the Invisible, Harry Beckwith. New York: Warner Books, 1997.

> Beckwith enriches the marketing mind with insight after insight simultaneously confirming conventional wisdom and exploding it. Focused on service marketing, the many for-profit examples are easily translatable to the nonprofit world. Written in bite-size chunks—consider it your daily marketing affirmation book.

The Seven Faces of Philanthropy, Russ Alan Prince and Karen Maru File. San Francisco: Jossey-Bass Publishers, 1994.

> Prince and File do a wonderful job segmenting major donors into seven categories based on psychographic profiles; in other words, they provide seven reasons why big givers give. In addition to being enlightening on its specific topic, this book is a wonderful reminder that every successful exchange relationship is founded on understanding and respect.

The Tao of Sales, E. Thomas Behr, Ph.D. Boston, MA: Element Books, Inc., 1997.

> If marketing poses a challenge to your meditation routine—or seems otherwise divorced from a holistic approach—enjoy a slant on sales that travels across continents and cultures to bring the wisdom of the ages to an approach based on harmony.

Worksheets

Electronic versions of these worksheets may be downloaded from the publisher's web site. Use the following URL and access code (case sensitive) to obtain the worksheets:

www.FieldstoneAlliance.org/worksheets

Access code: W253mW101

These online worksheets are intended for use in the same way as photocopies of the worksheets, but they are in a form that allows you to type in your responses and reformat the worksheets to fit your collaboration. Please do not download the worksheets unless you or your organization has purchased this workbook.

In what categories will you set marketing goals?

❑ Participation in programs, services, or events   ❑ Membership

❑ Enrollment   ❑ Sales of tickets, books, or other items

❑ Volunteer recruitment   ❑ In-kind contributions

❑ Funding   ❑ Other _____

_____

Use the following process to set your specific marketing goals.

Responses to questions 1–3 below should be brainstormed: that is, every answer is acceptable, even if they conflict.

You should make a clear decision on question 4. You may have one or more goal categories. Make copies of this worksheet and repeat these steps for *each* goal you want to set.

1. **What are the ideal results you could achieve?**

   First, define the categories of exchanges you want to make: funds, volunteers, members, in-kind contributions, and so forth, as listed in the columns at the top of this worksheet. Within each category you may have more than one goal. For example, if your goal category is funding, you might want specific results in major gifts, direct mail, and foundation grants. You might have a second goal category of in-kind contributions, with results specified in supplies, raffle prize donations, and computers.

   Now think big: if everything goes perfectly, what could the results be? (A little dreaming is fine at this point.)

Goal category	Ideal results (how much of what by when)

     (continued)

Goal category	Ideal results (how much of what by when)

2. What argues in favor of your ability to achieve these ideal results?

Think about factors inside the organization as well as those outside.

Inside factors working for us	*Outside* factors working for us

(continued)

3. What argues against your ability to achieve these results?

Now think about factors, inside and outside, that might hold you back.

Inside factors working against us	*Outside* factors working against us

4. What are your realistic, achievable goals? By when?

Try for consensus on this question.

a. Reflect on the internal and external factors, and then take a quick "gut-response" poll.
b. Discuss people's gut responses and attempt to arrive at a consensus. If you can't agree, draft low-end and high-end goals for now.

Achievable goal	By when

SECTION A—Check in with your mission

1. Write your current mission statement here:

   a. Is the mission clear and concise?

   b. Does it address the organization's opportunities, competence, and commitment?

   c. Does it provide the right direction for the future?

2. What changes, if any, should be considered in your mission?

(continued)

SECTION B—Look at needs and results

For information to complete this section, turn first to your customers and staff. They're the best sources you have: however, sometimes staff and customers are too close to issues and current programs to see what changes could produce even greater impact. Add some outside perspective too.

1. **List the most significant ongoing or emerging needs and opportunities you will address.**

2. **What are your results?**

SECTION C—Assess the environment to see how you fit in

1. Who else addresses issues within the scope of your mission—both on the ground and on the web?

2. Who competes directly with you?

3. What strengths do you bring to both collaboration and competition?

(continued)

SECTION C—Assess the environment to see how you fit in (continued)

   4. List potential partners and how you might team up with each.

There are four general ways your "fit" in the environment affects decisions on positioning.
How do things look for you? Check all those that apply:

❏ There are opportunities to make a unique contribution, and we're exactly the people to do the job.
   Comments:

❏ It will be best to pursue results through partnerships and collaboration.
   Comments:

❏ We need to be strongly competitive to meet needs and get results.
   Comments:

❏ The needs and opportunities we identified can be better addressed by others; we should back off.
   Comments:

SECTION D—Draft your positioning statement

Your positioning statement should make it easy for people to quickly grasp who you are and what unique role you want to play.

1. **To develop material for your statement, first complete the following phrases in as many ways as you can think of. (Instructions for structured ways to generate ideas are provided in Appendix A.)**

   a. We're the people who...

   b. No one but no one can _____ as well as we do.

(continued)

SECTION D—Draft your positioning statement (continued)

c. We want to be seen as...

2. **Now go back and circle the phrases that most strongly convey your niche and the reputation you want to build.**

3. **Based on the circled phrases in Section D, and applying the four criteria for positioning statements** *(short and to the point, uses everyday language, conveys character, and has a sense of action),* **write your draft statement here:**

SECTION E—Test your positioning statement for support

1. **List at least five (or more) key potential sources of support with whom you will test your positioning statement.**

2. **Make appointments with these key sources of support and, in each case, gain answers to these four questions:**

   a. Based on your knowledge of our organization and this community, do you agree this is how we should be positioned?

   b. Why or why not?

   c. How might we modify our ideas to improve them?

   d. Are there other people or groups you would recommend we talk with?

(continued)

SECTION F—Refine and clarify your positioning statement

Write your revised positioning statement here:

SECTION A—Product *What you offer*

1. What is the product?

2. Do you deliver value?

3. Is there anything about the product that makes it difficult to understand or use?

4. Do your customers give the product high marks?

✓ *Product Checkpoint*
   Is your product in line? Is it of high quality and does it deliver value?

   ❏ OK   ❏ Need information   ❏ Adjustment necessary   ❏ Benefit to promote

   Write your questions, adjustments needed, and promotion notes on Worksheet 4.

(continued)

SECTION B—Publics　*Those with whom you want to make exchanges; target audiences*

1. **Brainstorm a complete list of publics based on each marketing goal.**

SECTION B—Publics (continued)

2. **Choose your target audiences for each product and note the benefits of the product they value most.**

Target Audiences	Benefits

✓ *Publics Checkpoint*

Are your publics in line? Do you have the right target audiences and know the benefits most important to them?

❏ OK   ❏ Need information   ❏ Adjustment necessary   ❏ Benefit to promote

Write your questions, adjustments needed, and promotion notes on Worksheet 4.

(continued)

SECTION C—Price   *What you ask for in the exchange*

1. **What are you asking for? Dollars and cents or something else?**

2. **How much do you charge?**

3. **Could your customers—or at least some of them—pay more?**

✓ *Price Checkpoint*
   Is your price in line? Not too high and not too low for the value you deliver?

   ❏ OK   ❏ Need information   ❏ Adjustment necessary   ❏ Benefit to promote

Write your questions, adjustments needed, and promotion notes on Worksheet 4.

SECTION D—Place *Where the product is available*

1. Do people come to you or do you deliver the product where they are?

2. Are there any place "barriers" you should address?

✓ *Place Checkpoint*
    Is place in line? Is the product easily accessible to your target audiences?

❏ OK   ❏ Need information   ❏ Adjustment necessary   ❏ Benefit to promote

Write your questions, adjustments needed, and promotion notes on Worksheet 4.

(continued)

SECTION E—Production   *The ability to meet demand and serve customers well*

1. **Can you effectively meet demand?**

2. **What if demand increases—or falls?**

3. **Do you have standards and skills that delight every customer every time?**

✓ *Production Checkpoint*
    Is production in line? Can you effectively meet demand and serve customers well?

❑ OK   ❑ Need information   ❑ Adjustment necessary   ❑ Benefit to promote

Write your questions, adjustments needed, and promotion notes on Worksheet 4.

SECTION F—Promotion   *What you do to convey your image and motivate people to respond*

1. Image: How you want to be known

    a. What do you want your image to be?

    b. Do your promotion materials and techniques reflect the reputation you want to build?

    c. Does the image you want to convey strike the right chord with your target audiences?

✓ *Promotion Checkpoint*
   Do you convey the image you want?

❑ OK   ❑ Need information   ❑ Adjustment necessary   ❑ Benefit to promote

Write your questions, adjustments needed, and promotion notes on Worksheet 4.

    (continued)

SECTION F—Promotion (continued)

2. **What promotion techniques have you used? (See Appendix C for annotated list of techniques.) Note the effectiveness of each by placing a check in the appropriate column and add any comments you have.**

Technique	Produces good response	Conveys image we want	Speaks language of target audience

SECTION F—Promotion (continued)

3. What should you add, drop, or improve?

Add:

Drop:

Improve:

✓ *Promotion Checkpoint*
  Is promotion in line? Do you use effective techniques and tools that motivate people to respond?

❑ OK   ❑ Need information   ❑ Adjustment necessary   ❑ Benefit to promote

Write your questions, adjustments needed, and promotion notes on Worksheet 4.

SECTION A—Information Needed

If you checked *need information* in any of the sections on Worksheet 3, write the specific questions you want answers to below:

(continued)

SECTION B—Adjustments Necessary

If you checked *adjustment necessary* in any of the sections on Worksheet 3, note the specific problems needing attention below:

SECTION C—Promotion Notes

If you checked *benefit to promote* in any of the sections on Worksheet 3 or have other notes on promotion that come up during the audit, elaborate below:

SECTION A—Marketing Goals

Write your marketing goals here:

(continued)

SECTION B—The Plan

1. The product is:	Comments:

SECTION B—The Plan (continued)

2. **It will be marketed to these target audiences who value particular benefits:**

Target audiences (by goal category):	Benefit:	Comments:

(continued)

SECTION B—The Plan (continued)

3. At this price:	Comments:

4. Available at these locations:	Comments:

SECTION B—The Plan (continued)

5. To effectively meet demand and serve customers well, we will	Comments:

(continued)

SECTION B—The Plan (continued)

6. The major benefits to promote are:	Comments:

SECTION B—The Plan (continued)

7. Our basic approach to promotion will include:	Comments:

(continued)

SECTION C—Implementation

Step	Responsibility	Deadline	Budget

SECTION A—Image

An effective image makes the impression you want.

1. **Brainstorm a list of colorful and descriptive words or phrases, metaphors, or comparisons that reflect your desired image.**

2. **Circle the above items that do the best job of reflecting your desired image.**

Copyright © 2001 Fieldstone Alliance   *(continued)*

SECTION B—Message

An effective message prompts your target audience to take a specific action and promises a valuable benefit if they do.

1. Who is the target audience?

2. How do they best receive information—language and sources?

SECTION B—Message (continued)

3. What are the three key benefits of your product that target audiences value most?

4. What are the top features and options?

5. What is the call to action?

(continued)

SECTION C—Materials and Techniques

The principles for an effective combination are:

(1) Gear tools to the audience.
(2) Plan how each tool can be used to maximum effect.
(3) Pick the right mix—within budget.
(4) Frequency over time equals reach.

(5) If it worked, do it again.
(6) Don't abandon the basics.
(7) Stay the course.

Make the choices you believe will be most effective, keeping in mind budget constraints and how much effort you can realistically put into development and follow-through.

1. **Check the promotion tools you will use in your campaign.**

- ❏ Advertising
- ❏ Annual reports
- ❏ Atmosphere and attitude
- ❏ Billboards/transit ads
- ❏ Brochures
- ❏ Business cards, letterhead, and other essentials
- ❏ Celebrity endorsements
- ❏ Direct mail
- ❏ Editorials
- ❏ E-mail and fax

- ❏ Feature stories
- ❏ Letters to the editor
- ❏ Marketing partnerships
- ❏ Networking
- ❏ News conference
- ❏ News releases
- ❏ Newsletters
- ❏ Personal contact
- ❏ Posters
- ❏ Presentations, public speaking, and training

- ❏ Public service announcements
- ❏ Publishing articles and reports
- ❏ Signage
- ❏ Special events
- ❏ Specialty advertising
- ❏ Talk shows
- ❏ Telemarketing
- ❏ Trade fairs
- ❏ Videos
- ❏ Web site
- ❏ Word of mouth

2. **How will these materials and techniques work together to gain the response you want?**

SECTION D—Implementation

Step	Responsibility	Deadline	Budget

More results-oriented books from Fieldstone Alliance

Board Tools

The Best of the Board Café
Hands-on Solutions for Nonprofit Boards

by Jan Masaoka, CompassPoint Nonprofit Services

Gathers the most requested articles from the e-newsletter, *Board Café*. You'll find a lively menu of ideas, information, opinions, news, and resources to help board members give and get the most out of their board service.

232 pp   2003   ISBN 978-0-940069-40-4   Item #069407

Collaboration

Collaboration Handbook
Creating, Sustaining, and Enjoying the Journey

by Michael Winer and Karen Ray

Shows you how to get a collaboration going, set goals, determine everyone's roles, create an action plan, and evaluate the results. Includes a case study of one collaboration from start to finish, helpful tips on how to avoid pitfalls, and worksheets to keep everyone on track.

192 pp   1994   ISBN 978-0-940069-03-9   Item #069032

Collaboration: What Makes It Work, 2nd Ed.

by Paul Mattessich, PhD, Marta Murray-Close, BA, and Barbara Monsey, MPH

An in-depth review of current collaboration research. Major findings are summarized, critical conclusions are drawn, and twenty key factors influencing successful collaborations are identified. Includes The Wilder Collaboration Factors Inventory, which groups can use to assess their collaboration.

104 pp   2001   ISBN 978-0-940069-32-9   Item #069326

The Fieldstone Alliance Nonprofit Guide to
Forming Alliances: Working Together to Achieve Mutual Goals

by Linda Hoskins and Emil Angelica

This guide will help you understand and strategically form alliances that work at a lower level of intensity.

112 pp   2005   ISBN 978-0-940069-46-6   Item #069466

The Nimble Collaboration
Fine-Tuning Your Collaboration for Lasting Success

by Karen Ray

Shows you ways to make your existing collaboration more responsive, flexible, and productive. Provides three key strategies to help your collaboration respond quickly to changing environments and participants.

136 pp   2002   ISBN 978-0-940069-28-2   Item #069288

Community Building

Community Building: What Makes It Work

by Wilder Research Center

Reveals twenty-eight keys to help you build community more effectively. Includes detailed descriptions of each factor, case examples of how they play out, and practical questions to assess your work.

112 pp   1997   ISBN 978-0-940069-12-1   Item #069121

Community Economic Development Handbook

by Mihailo Temali

A concrete, practical handbook to turning any neighborhood around. It explains how to start a community economic development organization, and then lays out the steps of four proven and powerful strategies for revitalizing inner-city neighborhoods.

288 pp   2002   ISBN 978-0-940069-36-7   Item #069369

Community Leadership Handbook

by James F. Krile with Gordon Curphy and Duane R. Lund

Leadership is a choice, not a position. You can improve your community, and this hands-on guide shows you how. Based on the best of Blandin Foundation's 20-year experience in developing community leaders, it gives community members—like yourself—the tools to bring people together to make changes.

216 pp   2006   ISBN 978-0-940069-54-1   Item #069547

The Fieldstone Alliance Nonprofit Guide to
Conducting Community Forums

by Carol Lukas and Linda Hoskins

Provides step-by-step instruction to plan and carry out exciting, successful community forums that will educate the public, build consensus, focus action, or influence policy.

128 pp   2003   ISBN 978-0-940069-31-2   Item #069318

The Creative Community Builder's Handbook

by Tom Borrup

Art and culture can be a powerful catalyst for revitalizing the economic, social,and physical conditions in communities. This handbook gives you successful strategies, best practices, and "how-to" guidance to turn cultural gems into effective community change.

280 pp   2006   ISBN 978-0-940069-47-3   Item #069474

Crossing Borders, Sharing Journeys

Effective Capacity Building with Immigrant and Refugee Groups

by Sarah Gleason

This report outlines seven broad factors found to contribute to effective capacity building with immigrant and refugee lead organizations (IRLOs). Case studies illustrate practices used when working with IRLOs. You can also download a free copy of this report at www.FieldstoneAlliance.org.

88 pp   2006   ISBN 978-0-940069-62-6   Item #069628

New Americans, New Promise

A Guide to the Refugee Journey in America

by Yorn Yan

Gain a better understanding of the refugee experience in the U.S. Refugee-serving organizations will find practical advice for how to best help refugees through the acculturation and transition process of becoming a New American. Refugees will discover what to expect during five stages of development that they typically progress through as they adapt to their new home.

200 pp   2006   ISBN 978-0-940069-50-3   Item #069504

Finance

Bookkeeping Basics

What Every Nonprofit Bookkeeper Needs to Know

by Debra L. Ruegg and Lisa M. Venkatrathnam

Complete with step-by-step instructions, a glossary of accounting terms, detailed examples, and handy reproducible forms, this book will enable you to successfully meet the basic bookkeeping requirements of your nonprofit organization—even if you have little or no formal accounting training.

128 pp   2003   ISBN 978-0-940069-29-9   Item #069296

Coping with Cutbacks

The Nonprofit Guide to Success When Times Are Tight

by Emil Angelica and Vincent Hyman

Shows you practical ways to involve business, government, and other nonprofits to solve problems together. Also includes 185 cutback strategies you can put to use right away.

128 pp   1997   ISBN 978-0-940069-09-1   Item #069091

Financial Leadership for Nonprofit Executives

Guiding Your Organization to Long-term Success

by Jeanne Bell and Elizabeth Schaffer

Provides executives with a practical guide to protecting and growing the assets of their organizations and with accomplishing as much mission as possible with those resources.

144 pp   2005   ISBN 978-0-940069-44-2   Item #06944X

Venture Forth!

The Essential Guide to Starting a Moneymaking Business in Your Nonprofit Organization

by Rolfe Larson

The most complete guide on nonprofit business development. Building on the experience of dozens of organizations, this handbook gives you a time-tested approach for finding, testing, and launching a successful nonprofit business venture.

272 pp   2002   ISBN 978-0-940069-24-4   Item #069245

Funder's Guides

Community Visions, Community Solutions

Grantmaking for Comprehensive Impact

by Joseph A. Connor and Stephanie Kadel-Taras

Helps foundations, community funds, government agencies, and other grantmakers uncover a community's highest aspiration for itself, and support and sustain strategic efforts to get to workable solutions.

128 pp   2003   ISBN 978-0-940069-30-5   Item #06930X

A Funder's Guide to Evaluation

Leveraging Evaluation to Improve Nonprofit Effectiveness

by Peter York

This book includes strategies and tools to help grantmakers support and use evaluation as a nonprofit organizational capacity-building tool.

160 pp   2005   ISBN 978-0-940069-48-0   Item #069482

A Funder's Guide to Organizational Assessment

Tools, Processes, and Their Use in Building Capacity

Editor: Lori Bartczak

This guide presents four grantee assessment tools and two tools for assessing foundation performance.

216 pp   2005   ISBN 978-0-940069-53-4   Item #069539

Power in Policy

A Funder's Guide to Advocacy and Civic Participation

Editor: David F. Arons

Foundations are finding that participation in public decision making is often a critical component in reaching the impact they seek. For those weighing precisely what role foundations should play, the mix of real-life examples, practical advice, and inspiration in this book are invaluable.

320 pp   2007   ISBN 978-0-940069-45-9   Item #069458

Strengthening Nonprofit Performance

A Funder's Guide to Capacity Building

by Paul Connolly and Carol Lukas

This practical guide synthesizes the most recent capacity building practice and research into a collection of strategies, steps, and examples that you can use to get started on or improve funding to strengthen nonprofit organizations.

176 pp   2002   ISBN 978-0-940069-37-4   Item #069377

Lobbying & Advocacy

The Lobbying and Advocacy Handbook for Nonprofit Organizations

Shaping Public Policy at the State and Local Level

by Marcia Avner

The Lobbying and Advocacy Handbook is a planning guide and resource for nonprofit organizations that want to influence issues that matter to them. This book will help you decide whether to lobby and then put plans in place to make it work.

240 pp   2002   ISBN: 978-0-940069-26-8   Item #069261

The Nonprofit Board Member's Guide to Lobbying and Advocacy

by Marcia Avner

Written specifically for board members, this guide helps organizations increase their impact on policy decisions. It reveals how board members can be involved in planning for and implementing successful lobbying efforts.

96 pp   2004   ISBN: 978-0-940069-39-8   Item #069393

Management & Planning

The Accidental Techie

Supporting, Managing, and Maximizing Your Nonprofit's Technology

by Sue Bennett

How to support and manage technology on a day-to-day basis including: setting up a help desk, developing an effective technology budget and implementation plan, working with consultants and management, handling viruses, creating a backup system and schedule, purchasing hardware and software, and more.

176 pp   2005   ISBN 978-0-940069-49-7   Item #069490

Benchmarking for Nonprofits

How to Measure, Manage, and Improve Results

by Jason Saul

This book defines a formal, systematic, and reliable way to benchmark (the ongoing process of measuring your organization against leaders), from preparing your organization to measuring performance and implementing best practices.

144 pp   2004   ISBN 978-0-940069-43-5   Item #069431

Consulting with Nonprofits: A Practitioner's Guide

by Carol A. Lukas

A step-by-step, comprehensive guide for consultants. Addresses the art of consulting, how to run your business, and much more. Also includes tips and anecdotes from thirty skilled consultants.

240 pp   1998   ISBN 978-0-940069-17-6   Item #069172

The Fieldstone Alliance Nonprofit Guide to Crafting Effective Mission and Vision Statements

by Emil Angelica

Guides you through two six-step processes that result in a mission statement, vision statement, or both. Shows how a clarified mission and vision lead to more effective leadership, decisions, fundraising, and management. Includes tips, sample statements, and worksheets.

88 pp   2001   ISBN 978-0-940069-27-5   Item #06927X

The Fieldstone Alliance Nonprofit Guide to Developing Effective Teams

by Beth Gilbertsen and Vijit Ramchandani

Helps you understand, start, and maintain a team. Provides tools and techniques for writing a mission statement, setting goals, conducting effective meetings, creating ground rules to manage team dynamics, making decisions in teams, creating project plans, and developing team spirit.

80 pp   1999   ISBN 978-0-940069-20-6   Item #069202

The Five Life Stages of Nonprofit Organizations

Where You Are, Where You're Going, and What to Expect When You Get There

by Judith Sharken Simon with J. Terence Donovan

Shows you what's "normal" for each development stage which helps you plan for transitions, stay on track, and avoid unnecessary struggles. This guide also includes The Wilder Nonprofit Life Stage Assessment to plot and understand your organization's progress in seven arenas of organization development.

128 pp   2001   ISBN 978-0-940069-22-0   Item #069229

Generations

The Challenge of a Lifetime for Your Nonprofit

by Peter Brinckerhoff

What happens when a management team of all Baby Boomers leaves within a five year stretch? The clock is ticking....is your nonprofit ready? In this book, nonprofit mission expert Peter Brinckerhoff tells you what generational changes to expect and how to plan for them. You'll find in-depth information for each area of your organization—staff, board, volunteers, clients, marketing, technology, and finances.

232 pp   2007   ISBN 978-0-940069-55-8   Item #069555

Information Gold Mine

Innovative Uses of Evaluation

by Paul W. Mattessich, Shelly Hendricks, Ross VeLure Roholt

Don't underestimate the power of your evaluation findings. The real-life stories in this book clearly show the usefulness of evaluation data to produce good things for your nonprofit.

128 pp   2007   ISBN 978-0-940069-51-0   Item #069512

The Manager's Guide to Program Evaluation:

Planning, Contracting, and Managing for Useful Results

by Paul W. Mattessich, PhD

Explains how to plan and manage an evaluation that will help identify your organization's successes, share information with key audiences, and improve services.

96 pp   2003   ISBN 978-0-940069-38-1   Item #069385

The Nonprofit Career Guide

How to Land a Job That Makes a Difference

by Shelly Cryer

Help recruit the next generation of nonprofit leaders. Get the facts about the sector, its prominence, and its scope. Use this information to dispel myths and point talent to nonprofit work.

300 pp   2008   ISBN 978-0-940069-59-6   Item #069596

The Nonprofit Mergers Workbook Part I, Updated Ed.

The Leader's Guide to Considering, Negotiating, and Executing a Merger

by David La Piana

Save time, money, and untold frustration with this highly practical guide that makes the merger process manageable. Includes case studies, decision trees, worksheets, and complete step-by-step guidance.

240 pp   2008   ISBN 978-0-940069-72-5   Item #069725

The Nonprofit Mergers Workbook Part II

Unifying the Organization after a Merger (includes CD-ROM)

by La Piana Associates

Mergers Part II helps you create a comprehensive plan to achieve integration—bringing together people, programs, processes, and systems into a single, unified whole.

248 pp   2004   ISBN 978-0-940069-41-1   Item #069415

Nonprofit Stewardship

A Better Way to Lead Your Mission-Based Organization

by Peter C. Brinckerhoff

You may lead a not-for-profit organization, but it's not your organization; it belongs to the community it serves. You are the steward—the manager of resources that belong to someone else. The stewardship model of leadership can help your organization improve its mission capability by forcing you to keep your organization's mission foremost.

272 pp   2004   ISBN 978-0-940069-42-8   Item #069423

The Nonprofit Strategy Revolution

Real-Time Strategic Planning in a Rapid-Response World

by David La Piana

This ground-breaking guide offers a compelling alternative to traditional strategic planning. You'll find new ideas for how to form strategies, and the tools and framework needed to infuse strategic thinking throughout your organization. The result: your nonprofit will be more strategic in thought and action on a daily basis. When the next opportunity (or challenge) comes along, you'll be able to respond swiftly and thoughtfully.

208 pp   2008   ISBN 978-0-940069-65-7   Item #069657

Resolving Conflict in Nonprofit Organizations

The Leader's Guide to Finding Constructive Solutions

by Marion Peters Angelica

Helps you identify conflict, decide whether to intervene, uncover and deal with the true issues, and design and conduct a conflict resolution process.

192 pp   1999   ISBN 978-0-940069-16-9   Item #069164

Strategic Planning Workbook for Nonprofit Organizations, Revised and Updated

by Bryan Barry

Chart a wise course for your nonprofit's future. This time-tested workbook gives you practical step-by-step guidance, real-life examples, one nonprofit's complete strategic plan, and easy-to-use worksheets.

120 pp   1997   ISBN 978-0-940069-07-7   Item #069075

Marketing

The Fieldstone Alliance Nonprofit Guide to
Conducting Successful Focus Groups

by Judith Sharken Simon

Shows how to collect valuable information without a lot of money or special expertise. Using this proven technique, you'll get essential opinions and feedback to help you check out your assumptions, do better strategic planning, improve services or products, and more.

80 pp   1999   ISBN 978-0-940069-19-0   Item #069199

Marketing Workbook for Nonprofit Organizations Volume II: Mobilize People for Marketing Success

by Gary J. Stern

Put together a successful promotional campaign based on the most persuasive tool of all: personal contact. Learn how to mobilize your entire organization, its staff, volunteers, and supporters in a focused, one-to-one marketing campaign. Comes with *Pocket Guide for Marketing Representatives*. In it, your marketing representatives can record key campaign messages and find motivational reminders.

192 pp   1997   ISBN 978-0-940069-10-7   Item #069105

Message Matters

Succeeding at the Crossroads of Mission and Market

by Rebecca Leet

Today being heard demands delivering information that resonates with your audience's desires quickly, clearly, and continually. Message Matters gives you a simple framework for developing and using strategic messages so you can connect more successfully with your target audiences and compel them to action.

160 pp   2007   ISBN 978-0-940069-63-3   Item #069636

www.ingramcontent.com/pod-product-compliance
Lightning Source LLC
Chambersburg PA
CBHW061325190326
41458CB00011B/3897